SHOES A–Z

Jonathan Walford

SHOES A–Z

Designers, Brands, Manufacturers and Retailers

Thames & Hudson

With 373 illustrations, 346 in color

Half-title page **JAN JANSEN**
Suede and kid sandal, 2009.
For Jan Jansen, see p. 123.

Frontispiece **CALDERONE SHOES**
Sunrise appliqué leather pumps, mid-1980s.
Calderone was purchased by Aldo in the 1990s.
For Aldo, see p. 16.

Right **SERGIO ROSSI**
Multi-colour leather peep-toe ankle boot,
Spring/Summer 2010.
For Sergio Rossi, see p. 208.

Opposite **IRREGULAR CHOICE**
Floral-trimmed 'Courtesan pink' pump, 2009.
For Irregular Choice, see p. 118.

For Maurice

Cover images courtesy Jonathan Walford, Seneca Fashion Resource Centre and Shoe Icons

First published in 2010 in hardcover in the United States of America by Thames & Hudson Inc., 500 Fifth Avenue, New York, New York 10110

thamesandhudsonusa.com

Library of Congress Catalog Card Number 2010923292

ISBN 978-0-500-51526-6

Printed and bound in China

CONTENTS

FOREWORD BY PETER FOX 6

INTRODUCTION: SHOES IN FASHION SINCE 1950 8

A–Z OF DESIGNERS, BRANDS, MANUFACTURERS AND RETAILERS 12

GLOSSARY: THE NAMING OF SHOES 246

ACKNOWLEDGMENTS AND SOURCES OF ILLUSTRATIONS 256

FOREWORD BY PETER FOX

I began my fifty-two-year career in the shoe business in Vancouver, Canada, working in a shoe shop owned by a Mr Sheppard. Mr Sheppard didn't believe in commissions; one way to earn extra was the manufacturer's ten-cent spif on every jar of Luxury polish sold. I would demonstrate Luxury's quality by polishing each customer's shoes at the fitting stool. When the manager retired his job slid over to me. I installed a shoeshine stand and a shine became a required finish on all non-suede and non-white buck sales.

I saw that an important part of designing was listening to influential customers and chatting up ideas with them, so that they became part of the creative process. If and when ideas turned into shoes, guess who became their greatest boosters? With such a fashionable, interactive clientele, I earned the reputation of having a prophetic fashion eye.

In 1970, when the skid road area of Vancouver was being gentrified into the vibrant shopping venue now known as Gastown, John Fluevog and I opened our first Fox and Fluevog store. The decor was based on the library scene from the 1938 Leslie Howard and Wendy Hiller film *Pygmalion*: we decorated with used books and antique furniture. An old-fashioned black leather, chrome, and white porcelain barber's chair stood prominently in our store, serving admirably as our shoeshine stand. The boutique became quite a celebrity magnet. One memorable day Robert Altman, Warren Beatty and Julie Christie flew in from Los Angeles to buy boots. I lost the coin toss and John got to polish Julie's boots as she lay back on the barber's chair. I polished Robert's and Warren's boots at the fitting stool, while they argued as to who had found the store first.

When we left the secure environment of our homely Vancouver shoe shop and were set loose in Canadian and European shoe factories, we required some kind of grounding device, so I kept in mind certain of our influential customers. I would try to share their thrill of wearing something totally new and original, and imagine what style they might be prepared to move on to next in order to maintain that high of new fashion. This ensured a natural progression from one season's avant-garde to the next. It seemed important that our shop should not carry any style that could be found elsewhere, so we attended all the major shoe shows – New York, Las Vegas, Düsseldorf, Milan, Bologna and London – to see what design niche remained unfilled and therefore open to us.

What characterized the 1960s and 1970s was an exciting Carnaby Street type of freedom that the young expressed in their clothing. Such freedom demanded fresh ideas, and any of us willing to feed this need succeeded in a way that was impossible before the late 1950s. Fashion designers could look back at what had gone before and predict what the future held. The shoe factories we worked with couldn't resist our know-nothing, upstart, wild and crazy ideas, and they made up for us all kinds of unusual footwear, from full D'Artagnan bucket boots to multi-coloured platforms.

By 1980 John and I had decided to go our separate ways, and the first Peter Fox Shoes shop opened in SoHo, which was then a little-known area of New York. I worked alongside my wife and co-designer Linda, whose flair for colour and texture turned some unusual styles into shoes that women just loved to wear. Our designs were influenced by the close fitting of the upper to the arch of the foot, emphasized in 1920s and 1930s fashion illustrations. I think there are few shapes equal to the beauty of the female shoe silhouette that hugs the foot up into the arch and down onto the vamp.

Rodolfo Orsini, who owned a shoe factory on the Adriatic Italian coast, responded to my excitement about the shape of the last and said he would like to make the Peter Fox line. At the last-maker's shop I was given a basic wooden last and ordered to demonstrate what I had been blabbering about. Visualize, if you can, a group of old-time Italian craftsmen sceptically looking on at this Canadian self-styled amateur designer, carving out the arch and re-shaping one of their standard forms. They measured the shank width and I heard 'non è possibile': it was only 30 mm wide, it must be 'un errore'. I insisted that it was no mistake, for the 30-mm shank was to be the distinctive character of the Peter Fox line. Derisively they christened me the '30-mm man'. The first Peter Fox shoes on the new lasts, with heels influenced by the historical Louis heel, received adulation from the model who did a fit test. Before long we had a collection of lasts and heels exclusively for the Peter Fox brand, and thanks to their shapes, our shoes became known for their comfort.

Although I have now retired, I continue to admire the fresh ideas of style and comfort being explored in today's shoe designs. Turning the pages of this beautiful book is both nostalgic and exciting: Jonathan has truly captured the energy and inspiration of sixty years of shoes in fashion.

INTRODUCTION SHOES IN FASHION SINCE 1950

In the early 1950s, style guides in women's magazines suggested an average of eight or nine pairs of shoes as essential for the well-dressed woman. She should have black, brown or navy pumps, a sturdy pair of leather walking oxfords or derbies, white shoes for summer, silver or gold evening sandals, loafers for casual wear, tennis shoes for active wear, bedroom slippers, and galoshes for cold and wet weather. Other styles and colours were available but these were considered luxuries for special occasion outfits. In September 2007 a poll conducted by the Consumer Reports National Research Center found American women had on average nineteen pairs of shoes, more than double what their grandmothers owned nearly sixty years earlier.

Increased prosperity since 1950 has allowed more women to spend more money on their shoes, and with the concurrent decline in the use of other accessories – hats, gloves, scarves, and even stockings – shoes became more important as a source of style. However, multiple styles and on-trend novelties sometimes create too much choice and lead to fashion confusion and unbridled consumerism. Fashion theorists will point to the women's liberation movement, the sexual revolution, globalization and our increasingly youth-influenced culture as dominant factors in the shaping of footwear fashion. Shoe designers searching for next season's must-have 'look' have repeatedly rifled through the footwear lexicon, reviving past favourites in new combinations. As a result, the style of women's footwear of the past sixty years has been a pendulum, swinging between extremes. Since 1950 the toes of shoes have been rounded, pointed and squared, and heels have been tall, short, thin and chunky. The progression of silhouettes, colours and details seen on the feet of catwalk models each season, or in the pages of fashion magazines, no longer represent all fashion footwear, any more than haute couture represents all fashionable clothing. Multiplicity is the new word in shoe design, and industrial, sport and orthopaedic boots, shoes and sandals have been adopted into the fashion wardrobe.

While men's athletic and casual footwear has also become increasingly fashion-conscious over the last sixty years, business attire has changed little. Like the business suit, the classic oxford has not strayed far from its 1950 definition. Men's dress footwear does not change at the same rate or for the same reasons as women's: a pair of bespoke shoes made by a master craftsman from a firm such as John Lobb or Bontoni carries as much prestige in a gentleman's wardrobe today as it did sixty years ago.

It could be argued that today's high-fashion footwear has more in common with art than practicality, but the predominance of style over function is the nature of fashion.

Fashion is born the moment design transcends purpose. But not all designs succeed: wearable novelties only become leading fashions when worn by a significant following.

A century ago durability and affordability were the goals of mass-produced boots and shoes. As hemlines rose above the ankle in the 1910s, however, footwear design became a focus. In the 1920s most leading shoe designers were working in Paris where they could produce elegant and beautiful shoes in small workshops for the same clients who frequented the salons of haute couture. The period between 1920 and 1950 was an age of invention in footwear. New designs were introduced almost every season: sandals, peep-toes, sling-backs, platforms, wedge heels, ankle straps... Even the rationing of leather during the Second World War stimulated creativity by necessitating the use of alternative materials such as rope, canvas, wood, oilcloth and cellophane.

The United States was the largest shoe-manufacturing nation at this time but rising labour costs in post-war America meant that mass-produced shoes were profitable only if made in high volume. The Italian shoe industry was organized in 1945 under the National Association of Italian Footwear Manufacturers. Smaller Italian shoe factories, with traditionally trained shoemakers who could combine their talent for hand-finishing with mechanized production, were better suited for making smaller runs of high-fashion footwear. Italian manufacturers were opening up in central-northern Italy, from Lombardy to the Marche region, and around the cities of Florence and Venice, where there was access to materials, machinery and skilled artisans. Italian footwear earned a reputation for quality and luxury, especially for the new thin 'stiletto' heeled shoes that became the fashion hit of the late 1950s and remained in style for a decade.

By 1968 fashion footwear had taken on a more youthful style with wide toes and small heels – a look inspired by what girls had worn in previous decades. That year also marked the beginning of an irreversible decline in shoe manufacturing in the United States. Italy was firmly established as the leader in women's luxury footwear production, but now the labels 'Made in Spain' and 'Made in Brazil' were beginning to appear in shoes as well. Alicante, in the southern province of Valencia, was the centre of the Spanish footwear industry. Lower wages in Spain created a cost advantage for Spanish footwear so that it could compete with other mid-priced footwear. By 1975 Spain had over 1,800 firms producing shoes for export. Brazil's shoe industry, centred in Rio Grande do Sul, began exporting only in 1968, but when rising wages made Spanish shoes less competitive in the late 1970s Brazilian exports picked up steam.

TRACEY NEULS
Shoes from the Spring/Summer 2010 collection. For Tracey Neuls, see p. 167

The 1970s was a decade of change in both the footwear industry and footwear styles. Brand name trainers outsold all other types of shoe, including platform shoes, which were popular with the young, and orthopaedic styles (negative-heeled shoes and contour footbed sandals) that found unexpected success. The trainers market brought a production boost to Asia, where there was a favourable balance between low labour costs and access to raw materials. However, rising labour costs during the 1980s in South Korea and Taiwan induced manufacturers to move production to Indonesia and China, and later Vietnam. China today has 40,000 businesses engaged in shoe production, about 15 per cent of which have gained a foothold in the fashion footwear market.

Today's market is brand driven. Designers like Maud Frizon, Andrea Pfister, Walter Steiger, Robert Clergerie, Manolo Blahník and Christian Louboutin have made some of the most desirable fashion statement shoes of the past thirty years, and the prestige of their labels has transformed their names into brands. In 1955 Christian Dior began crediting his shoe designer, Roger Vivier, alongside his own name on the label of Dior shoes. However, despite this precedent, credit is not usually given for the shoe designer who works under a manufacturer's or a fashion designer's name, and designer footwear carries no guarantee that the shoe was created by the person whose name appears on the lining. In 1957 a sling-back pump with a dark toecap was introduced at Chanel: shoemakers Raymond Massaro and René Mancini both take credit for this shoe design, but neither of their names ever appeared as part of this signature Chanel style. Fashion designers rely upon prêt-à-porter, scents, accessories and footwear to make profits for their businesses, avoiding dilution of the brand whenever possible. Outsiders' names are therefore usually omitted, making it impossible to know whether a design was created by the named designer, a freelance designer or an in-house design assistant. Similarly, shoe factories in Italy, Brazil, China and elsewhere make shoes under brand or retailers' names with no hint of who the manufacturer is other than the necessary legal requirement to state the country of origin. This became apparent in the 1990s when well-known European and American brands started being marked 'Made in China'.

By the 1990s fashion journalists were embracing vintage revival styles as eagerly as avant-garde designs that used neither traditional materials nor established construction techniques. Crossover styles have redefined the shoe lexicon, particularly since 2000: jewelled rubber flip-flops, stiletto-heeled trainers and sling-back oxfords have challenged traditional shoe types. The most recent trend in the footwear industry has been the adoption of eco-friendly recycled, renewable and sustainable materials from natural, organic and vegan sources.

t would be an impossible task to credit every designer, manufacturer, retailer and brand in the history of footwear. More than 50,000 companies are involved in footwear manufacturing today. In Italy alone there are over 6,400 firms, ranging from small workshops employing fewer than a dozen people to factories mass-producing shoes. This book focuses on the leading designers, manufacturers, retailers and brands of women's fashion footwear worldwide since 1950.

NORMA KAMALI
High-heeled rubber and cotton laced shoes, inspired by athletic footwear, and 'Made in China' for the Norma Kamali fashion brand, mid-1980s

"the look
of sandals in
flower
colours"
a.s. beck
fifth avenue shoes
This year's fashion for flowers is growing in a garden of new kidskin colours.
These fresh cut sandals are blooming with larkspur, magnolia,
and nasturtium colours, in new arrangements. Beck shoes from $6.99 to $10.95
148 stores in 40 major cities including
New York • Chicago • Miami • Palm Beach • Philadelphia • Washington • Detroit

A. S. BECK SHOE CORPORATION
Advertisement for A. S. Beck shoe stores, May 1956

ADRIANA CARAS
Fashion shot of stiletto-heeled sandals, Spring 2010

A. S. BECK SHOE CORPORATION

Alexander Samuel Beck's chain of retail shoe stores started in Brooklyn, New York, in 1909 but expanded rapidly after it was sold to investors in 1945. By the middle 1950s the company had about 150 locations east of the Rockies, but it began to shrink in the 1960s and the final store closed in 1982.

ADRIANA CARAS

Starting as a handbag designer in Los Angeles in the 1990s, Adriana Caras branched into shoes by 2000. Her ready-to-wear shoes and bags are made in Italy.

ADRIAN VIDAL

Manufacturer founded in the late 1980s in Elda, Spain, to produce high-fashion women's footwear for export to the UK, France, Italy, Russia and Nigeria.

AEROSOLES

Manufacturer founded in 1987 in Edison, New Jersey. The company aimed to create affordable and comfortable high-fashion footwear for working women. Brands include Aerosoles, What's What (a more fashion-forward line), A2 (basics and bestsellers), as well as Aerology, Sole A and Flexation.

AEROSOLES
'Cheery O' covered heel in red leather and suede with straps and buckles, 2009

ALAIN TONDOWSKI
Above **Perforated high heels in black and green leather, mid-2000s**

Opposite **Blue satin high heels with crisscross design, mid-2000s**

ALAIN TONDOWSKI

Born in 1968, Tondowski studied at Studio Berçot in Paris, before becoming a design assistant at **STEPHANE KÉLIAN** in 1989. The following year he joined Christian Dior, where he remained until 1994. He launched his own line of shoes in 1997 and has worked exclusively on his own collections since 2003.

ALBERTO ZAGO

Italian shoe manufacturer founded in 1965 by Luigi Zago. The company was named for his son Alberto, who is the current managing director.

ALDO

French-born Aldo Bensadoun began his career as a retailer of affordable, high-fashion footwear when, in 1972, he opened footwear concessions in a chain of fashion boutiques in Canada. The first Aldo store opened in Montreal and by 1993 the company had 95 shoe stores across Canada. In that year Aldo opened its first American store in Boston, and in 1994 its first international store in Israel. Aldo now has 900 retail stores and franchises throughout North America, Europe, Australia and the Middle and Far East. The company also created the brands Simard & Voyer, Pegabo (which had its own shops), Transit and Stoneridge, but these brands have now been merged or rebranded under Aldo.

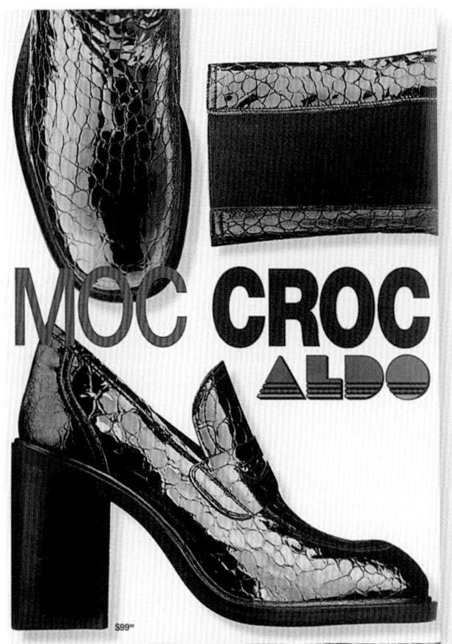

ALDO BRUÉ

Founded as a men's shoe manufacturer in 1946 by Mariano Brué in Marche, Italy, the company is now directed by his son, Aldo Brué, who is also its designer. A factory was built in 1968 to expand production for export and in the 1990s a woman's line was added, as well as a casual line called Attiva.

ALEXANDRA NEEL

After training as a ballerina, Alexandra Neel turned her talents to shoe design, learning her trade at the prestigious fashion houses of Celine, Balenciaga and Nina Ricci. Neel is often inspired by lingerie, using sensuous curves, lace and corsetry details in her shoe styles. Neel designed shoes for **CHARLES JOURDAN** in 2009, as well as her own collection, which is carried by luxury stores around the world.

ALDO

Left **Advertisement for Aldo, Autumn 1995**

Below **Advertisement for Aldo, Spring 1993**

AMALFI

The New York importers Marx & Newman created the Amalfi brand in 1946 for Italian shoes made by Rangoni, a Florentine manufacturer. In 1962 the **UNITED STATES SHOE CORPORATION (USSC)** bought out Marx & Newman, but the Amalfi name was retained by Rangoni's shoes until 1985. Thereafter USSC used the Amalfi name for any Italian footwear imported for resale under the Amalfi brand, resulting in a legal battle with Rangoni over the right to use the name.

AMARANTI

Manufacturer founded in 1973 in Civitanova Marche, Italy. Edoardo Amaranti designs for the women's trend market in fashion.

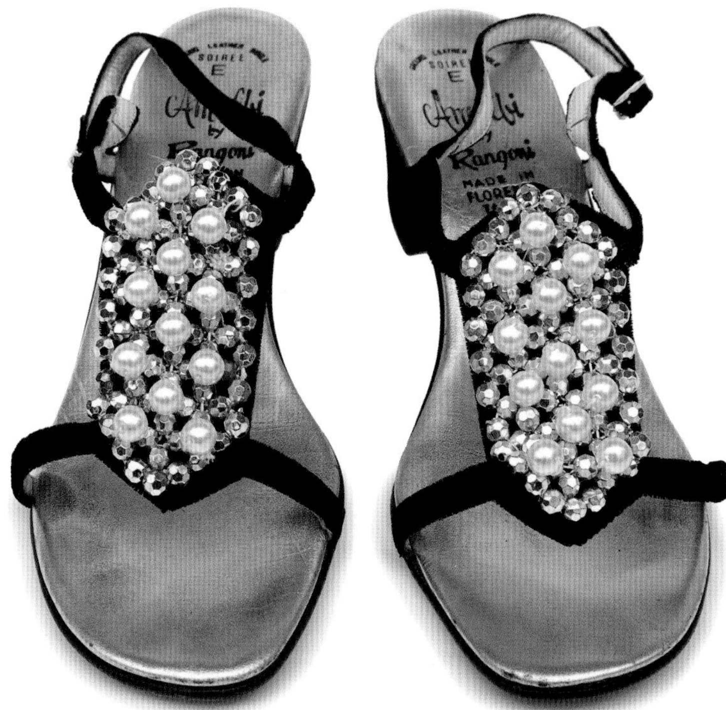

AMALFI
Black velvet and silver kid sandals decorated with faux pearls, *c.* 1968

ANDREA CARRANO

Andrea Carrano (1926–97) founded his Milan-based shoe company in the 1950s, and it gained fame for the production of ballerina flats. Andrea reached the peak of his influence in the early 1990s when he was making shoes for Krizia, Christian Dior, Michael Kors and Norma Kamali. The company lost ground in the 1990s recession and closed around the time of Andrea's death. His widow, Betta Carrano, relaunched Andrea Carrano shoes in December 2008.

ANDREA MORELLI

The women's fashion footwear collection Andrea Morelli was launched in autumn 2006. It is made and distributed by Calzaturificio Elisabet, a footwear company established in Monte Urano, Italy, in 1980.

ANDREA CARRANO

Above **Advertisement for Andrea Carrano, Spring 1986**

Left **Mesh pumps, late 1980s**

ANDREA PFISTER
Leather appliqué pumps, early 1980s

ANDREA PFISTER

Andrea Pfister was born in 1942 in Pesaro, Italy, and attended the Ars Sutoria shoe design school in Milan. In 1963 he won Best International Footwear Designer with a snakeskin pump entitled Comedie, and the following year he was designing footwear for Patou and Lanvin. In 1965 Pfister established his first eponymous collection, with which he and partner Pierre Dupré opened their first boutique in Paris at 4 rue Cambon. After expanding into handbags and belts, Pfister opened his second boutique in 1987 in Milan. The following year he was once again recognized as Best International Footwear Designer when he received the Grand Fashion Medal of Honor in New York, the first living designer ever to receive this award. From his studio in Positano, Italy, Pfister gathers his inspirations to create his twice-yearly collections. A master of colour and applied decoration, he is known for adorning his shoes with sumptuous displays of embroidery, sequins and exotic skins. As well as running his own line, Pfister has also designed for Anne Klein, Louis dell-Olio and **BRUNO MAGLI**. His footwear is reproduced under licences but the United States accounts for the majority of his business.

ANDRE ASSOUS

In the early 1970s importer Andre Assous and partner Jacques Cohen introduced to America the peasant espadrille style, a linen or hemp upper stitched to a wedge sole. It was perfect for the hippie chic of the period and has passed in and out of fashion ever since. Assous diversified to include men's footwear, leather footwear, a Featherweights light-sole shoe collection and, in 2000, a higher-end line of feminine and decorative shoes with matching bags called Collection.

ANDRÉ PERUGIA

André Perugia (1893–1977) was born in Tuscany, but moved with his family to Nice, where he learned shoemaking from his father. After the First World War, during which he worked as an aircraft engineer, in 1921 Perugia opened a shop at 11 Faubourg Saint-Honoré with the support of the fashion designer Paul Poiret, who introduced his clients to Perugia. He expanded to Nice in the mid-1920s, and in 1930 began collaborating with Elsa Schiaparelli. From 1937 until the end of his career his Paris shop was at 2 rue de la Paix. Perugia designed under his own label, as well as for **H. & R. RAYNE** in England and **I. MILLER** in the US, registering numerous patents, including one in 1956 for interchangeable heels. Throughout his prolific career Perugia drew inspiration for his shoes from the Orient, modern art, industrial design and history. From 1962 to 1966 he worked as a technical adviser for **CHARLES JOURDAN**, to which at his death he left his archive.

ANDREW GELLER

Just after the First World War the American retailer Andrew Geller introduced a wholesale line of women's shoes. As it grew, the family business incorporated other brands, most notably **JULIANELLI**. The company had its heyday in women's shoe designs in the 1950s and 1960s.

ANDRE ASSOUS
Advertisement for Andre Assous, Autumn 1993

ANDREW GELLER

Left Advertisement for Andrew Geller, Summer 1975

Below Cream and brown pumps, *c.* 1960

ANGIOLINI, ENZO

Italian-born Angiolini (1942–93) was recruited in 1978 by Marx & Newman, a division of **UNITED STATES SHOE CORPORATION**, as the exclusive designer for Bandolino. Both Bandolino and a later line named Enzo did well, in part because production was moved from Italy to Brazil. Bandolino and Enzo brands were top sellers on most retailers' lists during the 1980s.

APEPAZZA

Italian fashion shoes made by Moda Ruggi in Padua, Italy. They are imported into the US by **CONSOLIDATED SHOE** and sold under the label Apepazza.

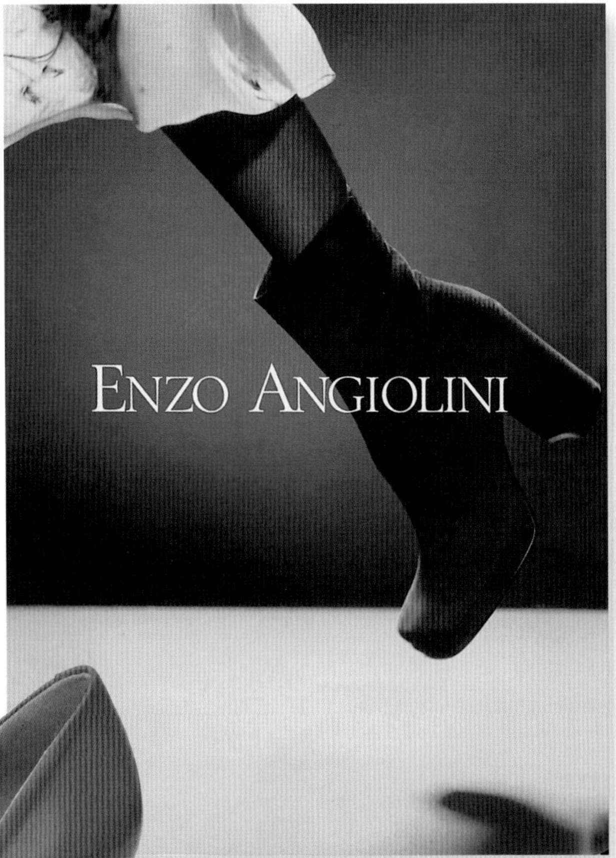

ENZO ANGIOLINI

ANGIOLINI, ENZO
Above **Advertisement for Enzo Angiolini, Autumn 1997**

Left **Pink leather pumps labelled Bandolino by Enzo Angiolini, mid-1980s**

ARCHE

Pierre Robert Hélaine learned to make wooden-soled shoes in Tours, France, during the Second World War. Remaining in the Loire Valley, in the 1950s he began making comfort shoes and moccasins with crêpe rubber soles. In 1968 Hélaine and his wife, Andrée, founded the Arche company. The brand entered the American and German markets in the early 1980s but expansion was slow until after Pierre's death in 1997. Now the company sells throughout the United States, Europe, Japan and especially China, where the brand is very popular. Arche shoes are made with an eye for fashion as well as comfort, social responsibility and eco-friendliness.

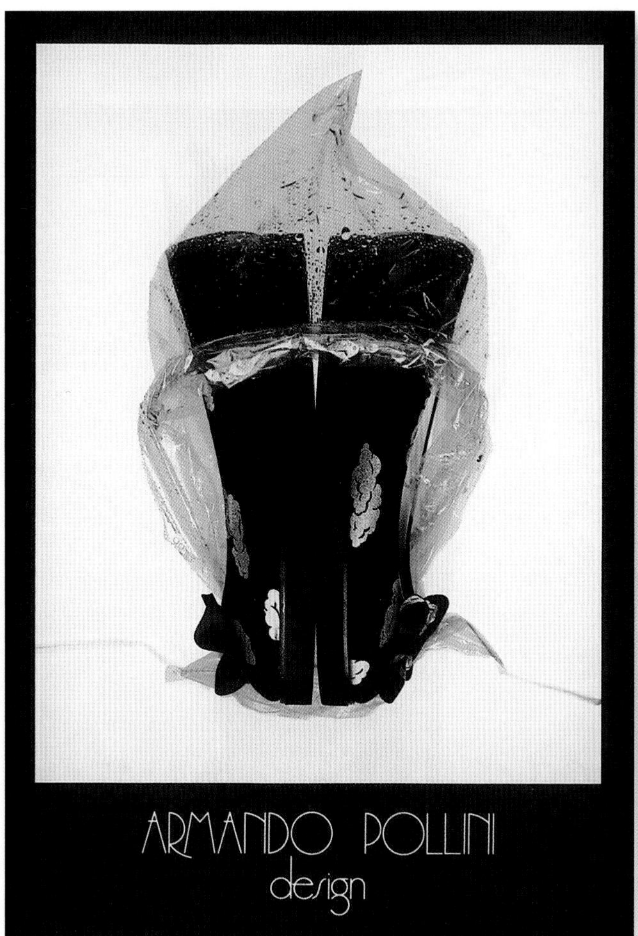

ARMANDO POLLINI
Advertisement for Armando Pollini, Spring 1986

ARCH PRESERVER *see* SELBY SHOE COMPANY

ARIKA NERGUIZ *see* MARANT

ARMANDO POLLINI

Armando Pollini was born in Italy in 1935 and worked in his father's pattern-making company (leaving briefly to train as a member of the Italian track and field team for the 1960 Olympics). In 1962 Pollini began work as a freelance designer for a variety of companies. He is among those credited with popularizing clogs and platforms in the early 1970s. In 1975 he created a clog consisting of a plastic bottom unit and leather strap. It was imported into the United States under the brand name **CANDIES** and became extremely popular in the late 1970s. Pollini's version of ballet flats were well known in the early 1980s. In the late 1980s he introduced a line of shoes with uppers made of elastic textile he called 'elast', that by the early 1990s accounted for 50 per cent of his company's sales.

ATTILIO GIUSTI LEOMBRUNI

Manufacturer founded in Montegranaro, Italy, in 1958 by Piero Giusti and currently under the direction of his son Attilio Giusti. Its shoes combine the artistry of hand-finishing with quality mechanized construction.

ATTILIO GIUSTI LEOMBRUNI
Hand-sewn soft lambskin moccasins with leather soles, 2010

ATTILIO GIUSTI LEOMBRUNI
Handmade patent leather sandals with leather soles, 2010

AUDLEY
Below **Purple and black oxford, Autumn 2009**

Opposite **White and metallic finish leather sandal, Autumn 2009**

AUDLEY

The company was founded in 1988 by Tim and Fiona Slack. Their Spanish-made shoe designs are conspicuously contemporary, following principles of architecture, especially the Bauhaus movement.

BALDININI

Manufacturer founded in 1910 and situated in the San Mauro Pascoli area on Italy's Adriatic coast. Gimmi Baldinini, the founder's grandson, took over the company in 1970. The name first came to international attention in 1974, when the company started to export the handmade mules that established the brand.

BALDININI
Advertisement for Baldinini, Autumn 1984

BALL BAND

The Mishawaka Rubber & Woolen Manufacturing Company took its name from the city in Indiana where it was founded in 1833. It developed a wide variety of products, from flannel underwear to galoshes. The factory's heyday was the turn of the twentieth century, when it trademarked Ball Band shoes. In 1934 the company introduced Summerettes, a style of cotton summer shoe with rubber soles that remained popular into the 1950s. However, after 1950 the manufacturing complex began to shrink, and in the 1960s Ball Band was acquired by Uniroyal and exists today only as a brand name.

BALL BAND
Advertisement for Ball Band, Autumn 1959

BALLCO

The manufacturer Calzados Ballester was founded in 1966 in Inca, Majorca, Spain. Under the brand name Ballco, the company produces fashion footwear for budget-conscious men and women in Spain and abroad.

BALLY

Carl Franz Bally began making footwear in Switzerland in the 1850s, and by the 1870s the company was making shoes largely for export. Carl Bally retired in 1892; his sons took over the business and set about making their product competitive on the high-end market. They started producing Goodyear-welted shoes and founded the London Shoe Company, to create better access to the market. Bally became a public company in 1907, and continued to grow and prosper into the 1960s.

In the 1950s Bally had added a line of hand-finished men's dress shoes, under the label Scribe. But by the late 1960s competition caused Bally's exports to decline and the company began to diversify its holdings and products. By 1976 it had added a ready-to-wear collection, handbags and leather accessories. The company left family ownership in 1977 and expanded rapidly in the 1980s, but sales began to falter in the 1990s with competitive brands taking a larger share of the luxury footwear market. In 1999 Bally was acquired by the US private investment firm Texas Pacific Group. Designer **BRIAN ATWOOD** was creative director from 2007–10, and was credited with rebuilding Bally's position as a leading luxury footwear manufacturer.

BALLY
Red low-heeled leather sling-back pump with pointed toe, mid-1960s

BANDOLINO *see* ANGIOLINI, ENZO

BANFI ZAMBRELLI

Silvano Banfi was born into a shoemaking family in Milan. In 1994 he emigrated to the United States and began designing for Calvin Klein, Banana Republic and Coach. While at Coach he met Frank Zambrelli, a graduate of the Fashion Institute of Technology in New York. Soon after Banfi and Zambrelli had launched Coach's shoe division, the two founded their own brand, designed in the US but made in Italy. They continue to design for other labels as well, including Judith Leiber, Calvin Klein and Nanette Lepore.

BASS

In 1876 George Henry Bass, a tanner, founded a company in Maine to make oiled leather hunting boots and camp moccasins. In 1936 it produced its version of a loafer using a stitching technique found on a Norwegian prototype, which gave the shoe its brand name, Weejun. In 1960 the *Daily Tarheel*, the student newspaper of the University of North Carolina, Chapel Hill, ran a headline, 'What are Bass Weejuns? – The thing on the feet of those who are with it.' Sales skyrocketed with the Ivy League set. In 1982 the men's shirt manufacturer Phillips-Van Heusen acquired Bass.

BATA

The Bata Shoe Company was founded by Tomas Bata in 1894 in Zlín, now in the Czech Republic. By the late 1920s, using American factory-line methods and machinery, the company had become the largest shoe manufacturer in Europe. Bata attempted to break into the United States, but the advent of the Second World War ended the company's plans to expand into a saturated market. After the war, the founder's son, also named Tomas, rebuilt the company's headquarters in London, and in 1964 moved its operations to Canada. From the 1950s into the 1970s Bata expanded into sixty-eight countries, as both manufacturers and retailers of its own-brand shoes. Never a leader in style,

BATA
Cream leather round-toed flat-heeled shoes, mid-1950s

Bata aimed to supply the demand for everyday footwear at affordable prices. Competition from discount retailers and cheaper imports caused the company to contract during the 1980s and 1990s, and in 2005 the Canadian stores were closed and the headquarters relocated to Lausanne, Switzerland. Bata remains family owned and now operates more than 5,000 retail stores. In addition to its own name brand, Bata is responsible for Marie Claire (women's fashion footwear), Power (athletic shoes) and Bubblegummers (for children). Athlete's World and Walking on a Cloud are both Bata-owned stores.

BATACCHI, PAOLO
Advertisement for Paolo Batacchi, Autumn 1997

BATACCHI, PAOLO

Batacchi graduated from the Ars Sutoria in Milan, and began designing shoes for a factory in Florence. In 1970, at the age of twenty-five, he became director of the Florence office of **GENESCO**, supervising marketing, production and design until 1979. The business side of the industry brought him into contact with **ANDREW GELLER**, and from 1980 to 1985 he designed shoes for his Geoffrey Beene's Beene Bag collection. In 1985 Batacchi was hired by the American shoe conglomerate Intershoe to launch Via Spiga. Named for the famous street in Milan, Via Spiga became the fashion footwear success story of the late 1980s and early 1990s. In 1988 Batacchi designed a lower-priced line called Studio Paolo and in 1991 a higher-priced couture line called V Spiga Couture. In 2005 Via Spiga was bought by the **BROWN SHOE COMPANY**, which hired Paola Venturi as the head designer for the label in January 2009.

BEA NOVELLI
Advertisement for Bea Novelli, Summer 2008

BEA NOVELLI

Swiss designer Bea Novelli's career as a custom shoemaker had a rocky start during the recession of the early 1990s. Her fortunes began to change when her design of a brocade printed mule was picked up by Saks and Bergdorf Goodman in New York, setting off a trend for mules not seen in the US since the 1950s Spring-o-lator craze (*see* **HERBERT LEVINE**). In 1997 Novelli began collaborating with a manufacturer near Milan, using microfibre uppers.

BEATRIX ONG
Advertisement for Beatrix Ong, Spring/Summer 2008

BELGIAN SHOES
Advertisement for Belgian Shoes, Spring 1958

BEATRIX ONG

Born in London in 1976, Beatrix trained in fashion and shoe design at Cordwainers College in London. She became the creative director at **JIMMY CHOO** in 1998 but launched her own label in 2002. In 2008 she introduced a line of men's shoes.

BELGIAN SHOES

Henri Bendel opened his first shoe shop in Manhattan in 1956, two years after he had sold the eponymous New York fashion store founded by his uncle. The shop offered handmade casual moccasins made in Belgium, hence Belgian Shoes. Henri Bendel died in 1997, at the age of eighty-nine, but the company continues to operate.

BELLE INTERNATIONAL

China's leading shoe retailer was started as a shoe wholesale manufacturer in 1991. Belle is the largest distributor in China of Nike, Adidas and **BATA**. It manufactures fashion brands under the labels Belle, Staccato and Joy & Peace. Two-thirds of its business is fashion footwear.

BELMONDO

Founded in Hamburg, Germany, in 1989, Belmondo produces a range of collections of men's and women's fashion and casual footwear. In recent years the company has attracted attention for its humourous advertising campaigns.

BENOÎT MÉLÉARD

By nature perhaps more an artist than a shoemaker, Benoît Méléard (born 1971) has created shoes that defy traditional definitions. He brought attention to his design ability in the middle 1990s, when he created a cloven-hoofed boot for a Jeremy Scott fashion show. Méléard has created shoes under his own label since 1998.

BELMONDO
Above left **Advertisement for Belmondo shoes, 2006**

Above **Advertisement for Belmondo shoes, 2009**

BERNARDO
Plastic jewel-trimmed thong sandals, mid-1960s

BERNARDO

Austrian-born Bernard Rudofsky worked as an architect, writer, professor, social historian and designer. He frequently lectured on the topic of modern fashion and his wife, Berta, taught courses on sandal-making. The couple were encouraged by the *Harper's Bazaar* editor Diana Vreeland, and from 1944 they made sandals that were featured in fashion shoots of clothes by Claire McCardell. The Rudofskys' designs were inspired by the simple styles of ancient Greek and Roman sandals. In 1947 Rudofsky founded the company Bernardo. It is most famous for its original classic, the Miami, which influenced the thong sandal as beachwear. Bernardo was one of the first American companies to employ Italian shoemakers. The company still thrives, and Bernardo shoes continue to be crafted by hand.

BETH LEVINE *see* **HERBERT LEVINE**

BEVERLY FELDMAN

Feldman graduated from New York's Pratt Institute as a footwear illustrator and designer in the 1970s and began designing glamorous shoes with playful ornamentation. She prides herself on being one of the few successful female shoe designers, and on actually working as a designer rather than simply lending her name to a product line. Her eponymous footwear and handbag company is based in Alicante, Spain, with distribution in nearly fifty countries.

BEVERLY FELDMAN
Below **Fruit appliqué pumps, early 1980s**

Opposite **Metallic kid and black suede pumps, early 1990s**

BILLI BI *see* **FRANSI**

BIRKENSTOCK

The German Birkenstock family has been making shoes since 1774. In 1964 Karl Birkenstock perfected a flexible, orthopaedic arch support with contoured cork footbeds. In 1967 Margot Fraser began importing Birkenstock sandals into the US, selling them through health stores. She set up her own import company, Footprint Sandals, five years later. In 1968 Josef and Helga Kanner acquired the Canadian distribution rights and sold the sandals through their Montreal-based company Serum International. The styles are differentiated by the arrangement of straps, and in 1973 the familiar two-strap Arizona was launched, which became the most popular North American brand for the next thirty years. Closed-toe mules called Boston clogs were introduced in 1977, and entirely closed shoes went on sale in 1985 under the brand Footprints. Sales of the sandals slumped in the 1980s but a faithful client base grew again in the 1990s. Birkenstock produces footwear under the brand names Tatami (begun in 1990), Papillio (1991), Birki (1993) and Betula (1994). In 1997 it opened its flagship store in San Francisco and in 2000 Birkenstock formed a licensing agreement with the estate of Grateful Dead guitarist Jerry Garcia to produce sandals decorated with his paintings. In 2005 Heidi Klum launched a line of Birkenstocks under her name.

BIRKENSTOCK
'Gizeh' style Birkenstocks with a cork/latex footbed and an adjustable strap in an array of colours, 2009

BLUNDSTONE

The company began in 1870 as an importer of English footwear into Tasmania. By the 1890s J. Blundstone & Co. were producing elastic-sided work boots in Hobart. Although originally designed as a work boot, the style became a popular street fashion in the late 1980s and 1990s. Since 2005 increasing production costs have forced the relocation of production to India and Thailand.

38 BIRKEN
245

BOCCACCINI

Shoe manufacturer founded in 1959 in the Marche region of Italy. The company grew through licensing collaborations with **PATRICK COX**, Alexander McQueen, Eva Mann and Max Mara, among others. In 1987 Alfredo Boccaccini created the brand L'Autre Chose (The Other Thing) which was immediately picked up by the clothier Barneys in New York. Michela Casadei was brought in as a designer of the line in 1998, followed a year later by Dutch designer Fredie Stevens, who created a new line for men called Red (later renamed Alfred).

BONNIE SMITH

Bonnie Smith is relatively unknown in shoe-design history because her name never appeared in the lining of a shoe. She graduated with a design degree in 1962 and three years later began as an assistant to the New York shoe designer **EVELYN SCHLESS**. Smith moved on to designing for **MARGARET JERROLD**, Kimel, Cherokee and **GAROLINI**, among others. In 1989 she began designing a low-cost high-volume shoe line for a Hong Kong manufacturer, but retired three years later.

BØRN

Company founded by Thomas McClaskie in the late 1990s which produces hand-sewn footwear using a traditional European Opanke construction. The sole is curved up around the foot, eliminating the need for glue to attach a sole for a waterproof seam. The shoes are promoted as eco-conscious because they don't use adhesives and they have fewer internal components. Also, the leathers used by the company are 'responsibly' tanned using a vegetable process (tanning can be highly polluting), resulting in an organic, recyclable product.

BØRN
Tall form-fitting boots in black leather, 2008

Paradise Shoes
WITH SMARTLY LOWER HEELS
SO RIGHT WITH FALL'S
BRIEF SKIRTS...
SO DIVINELY COMFORTABLE,
ALWAYS
All the way from medium to frankly low . . . these are shoes with a firm fashion footing, newly smart with everything you'll wear from morning through late-day. Three from a collection in suede or calf, from $12.95 at fine stores; write us, we'll tell you where. Brauer Bros. Shoe Co., Saint Louis.
TWA
WIN A FASHION FLING TO PARIS AND THE RIVIERA
...FROM PARADISE KITTENS
Additional prizes:
paradise
Kittens
BRAUER BROTHERS SHOE COMPANY • 4065 FOREST PARK BLVD. • ST. LOUIS, MISSOURI 63108

BRAUER BROTHERS
Above **Advertisement for Paradise brand shoes by Brauer Brothers, Autumn 1950**

Above right **Advertisement for Paradise Kittens brand shoes by Brauer Brothers, Spring 1965**

BRAUER BROTHERS

Brauer Brothers began in the late 1920s in St. Louis, Missouri, but the company was best known from the 1940s to the 1960s for its brands Paradise and Kittens. It lost ground to cheaper imports from Spain and Brazil in the 1970s. The company reorganized as Brauer Brothers Manufacturing, but is now no longer in business.

BRIAN ATWOOD

Left **'Rida' purple satin platform sandals, late 2000s**

Above **Grey suede ankle boots, late 2000s**

BROWN SHOE COMPANY
Advertisement for Air Step brand shoes by Brown Shoe Company, Autumn/Winter 1953

BRIAN ATWOOD

Atwood was born in Chicago in 1967 and graduated from the Fashion Institute of Technology, New York, in 1991 before becoming a model. In 1996 he started working at Versace in the diffusion Versus line. His own line of shoes was launched in 2001. Atwood was creative director of **BALLY** from 2007–10.

BRITISH SHOE CORPORATION *see* LILLEY & SKINNER

BROWN SHOE COMPANY

The Brown Shoe Company is a retailer, wholesaler and licenser of footwear. It has 900 American stores, mostly trading as Famous Footwear, and 400 more called Naturalizer, as well as a website, Shoes.com, which sells more than 150 brands. It began in 1878 when George Brown saw the potential of making shoes cheaply in St. Louis, Missouri. The enterprise grew rapidly and by 1893 George Brown had bought out his investors and renamed his business the Brown Shoe Company. The company prospered in the early years of the twentieth century, thanks to Richard Outcault's cartoon character Buster Brown, which was used to advertise the company's products. It created successful brands, such as Naturalizer (1927), Connie (1931) and LifeStride (1940). Brown entered the retailing business in 1950 by purchasing Wohl Shoes, a well-established St. Louis company. A number of other retail chains were added in the 1950s, including Regal Shoes (1953) and the giant G. R. Kinney (1956, which Brown was legally obliged to sell in 1962 for antitrust violations). The Canadian wholesale manufacturer Perth was added in 1959, Samuels Shoe Company in 1965, and the importer Italia Bootwear joined the Brown stable of companies in 1970. As the American shoe industry began to shrink after

1968, Brown bought clothing, sporting goods and toy companies, and in 1972 became the Brown Group Inc. As the company shifted from manufacturing to importing the name changed again, in 1984, to Brown Group International, and by 1988 only the profitable brands of Connie, Naturalizer and Buster Brown had been retained. Facing the changing American marketplace, Brown restructured, eliminating its American shoemaking plants in 1991, its Wohl retail chain in 1993, and its non-shoe holdings by 1995. In its concentrated form, Brown began to build its shoe brands again, acquiring Dr. Scholl's in 1991 and Larry Stuart (upscale women's shoes) in 1995. Important licensing agreements were made in 1996, with Adidas and with the proprietors of cartoon characters, from Barbie to Batman, which were put on children's shoes. In 1999 the Naturalizer brand was relaunched for a younger audience with more stylish designs and the company changed its name back to the Brown Shoe Company. In 2002 Brown launched the brand Carlos by Carlos Santana and in 2005 acquired the Bennett Footwear Group that included Franco Sarto and Via Spiga. In 2008 Brown launched celebrity licensed footwear for Reba McEntire, Fergie and Gretta Monahan. Other brands include Nickels and Etienne Aigner.

BRUNO BORDESE

Italian shoe designer Bruno Bordese, who is based in Milan, learned his trade in the 1980s working for fashion designers including Vivienne Westwood and Yohji Yamamoto. In 1995 he struck out on his own, creating lines of footwear under the labels Bruno Bordese and Clone. His collections follow youthful trends and vintage styling, borrowing heavily from 1970s and 1980s styles, but with a good dose of humour that results in a recognizable Bordese brand.

BRUNO FRISONI

Born in France to Italian parents in 1960, Bruno Frisoni learned his trade working for designers such as Scherrer and Lacroix. Frisoni launched his shoe collection in 1999 and became known for his feminine styling, which led to his appointment as the artistic director of **ROGER VIVIER** in 2004.

BROWN SHOE COMPANY
Advertisement for Marquise brand shoes by Brown Shoe Company, Spring 1968

MARQUISE®...THE SIGNATURE SHOE

Add the final touch of chic with a flourish of buckle and the new rising heel. From the Marquise Avant Garde collection. $18 to $22

WOHL SHOE COMPANY · SAINT LOUIS, MISSOURI · A Division of Brown Shoe Company

At Franklin Simon Stores; Lasalle's, Toledo; McKelvey's, Youngstown; Bressmer's, Springfield; Manchester's, Madison; Meier & Frank Company, Portland and Salem; and other leading stores.

BRUNO MAGLI
Metallic leather pumps, mid-1980s

BUTTERO
Calfskin riding style boot, designed *c.* 1980

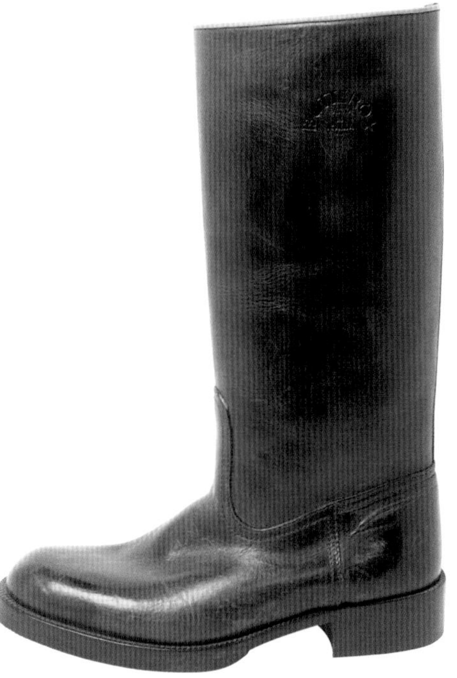

BRUNO MAGLI

Bruno Magli founded his company in Bologna in 1936, but it became well known only in the 1950s, when 'Made in Italy' became synonymous with quality and style. In the late 1960s Morris Magli, Bruno's nephew, became president and his wife, Rita, took over the creative direction. Rita has been credited with steering the company onto a more modern course and instigating Magli's association with designer **ANDREA PFISTER**. The company no longer belongs to the Magli family, but in 2005 it opened a museum of Bruno Magli's historical designs.

BUTTERO

Manufacturer founded in 1974 by Mauro Sani in Florence, Italy, creating men's and women's boot designs based on the tradition of the Tuscan cowboy.

CAFÉNOIR *see* **TOSCANA CALZATURE**

CAMILLA SKOVGAARD

Danish-born Camilla Skovgaard moved to Paris in her late teens to train as a couturier. After working in that role for seven years in Dubai, for the wives and daughters of sheikhs, she moved to London in 2000 to earn a degree in footwear at Cordwainers College. While working on her MA at the Royal College of Art she met shoe manufacturers from Italy and her eponymous shoe line was launched before she graduated in 2006, the same year that British fashion house Matthew Williamson appointed her its shoe designer.

CAMMINA *see* GEMINI GROUP

CAMPER

Spanish footwear company founded in 1975 by Lorenzo Fluxa, whose family had made shoes since 1877. Camper ('peasant' in Catalan) began with a rubber-tyre soled canvas shoe called Chameleon, and now specializes in casual day and sports shoes. At first available through multi-brand shoe retailers, Camper opened its flagship shop in Barcelona in 1981. In the late 1990s the company became an international leader in dressy sports-style shoes.

CAMPER
Floral-patterned canvas shoes with instep ties, 1990s

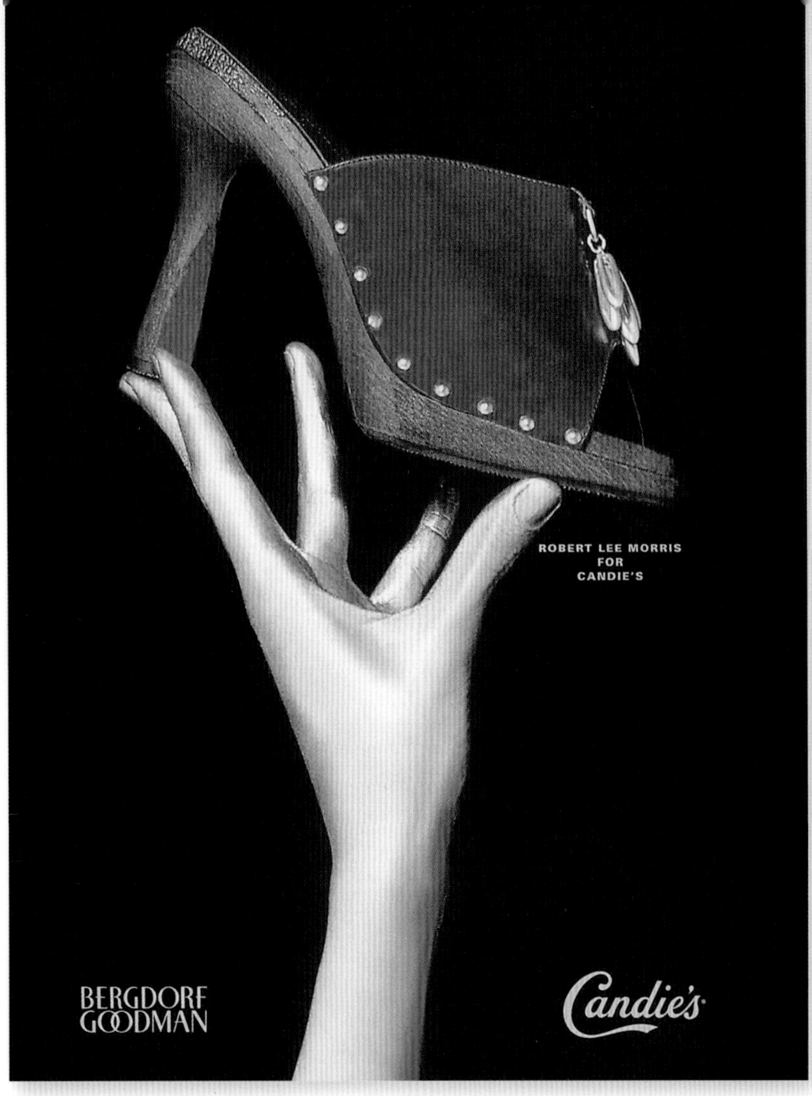

CANDIES
Advertisement for Candies, Spring 1998

CANDIES

A brand of clog designed in Italy by **ARMANDO POLLINI** and first imported into the US in 1978 by El Greco, a company operated by Charles Cole, the father of **KENNETH COLE**. Candies was founded in 1981 and was sold in 1993 to Iconix Brand Group who expanded the line to include accessories and scents.

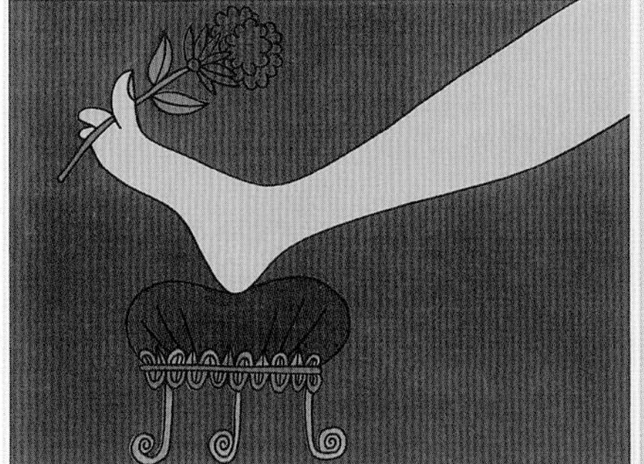

CAPARROS

Born in Puerto Rico, Anavel Caparros worked for eighteen years as a designer in Spain and Asia, before founding Caparros Shoes in 1988. She specializes in elegant evening styles and her shoes are sold through department stores and boutiques, as well as online.

CAPEZIO

Salvatore Capezio was born in Italy and emigrated to the USA, where he founded Capezio theatrical footwear in 1887. His store was fortunate in its New York city location, advantageously situated diagonally across the street from the Metropolitan Opera House, then at Broadway and 39th. While in New York during a tour in 1910, Anna Pavlova purchased Capezio pointe shoes for her entire company. In 1941 the young clothes designer Claire McCardell showed Capezio soft-soled ballet slippers with her collection. This prompted the Lord & Taylor department store to feature a line of low-heeled street-wear shoes built on dance footwear lasts, catapulting Capezio into the fashion footwear world. In the 1950s Capezio was known for popularizing toe cleavage in its low-cut shoes.

CAPEZIO

Above **Advertisement for Capezio, Autumn 1963**

Right **Purple cotton wedge-heeled pumps, late 1970s**

CARAS *see* **ADRIANA CARAS**

CARLISLE SHOE COMPANY

With its head office in the Empire State Building in New York, the Carlisle Shoe Company sought to reach the high-end fashion footwear market. Although the company dates back to the turn of the twentieth century, its most famous brand, Mademoiselle, began in 1937. The brand survived well after General Shoe bought it out in 1954.

CARLOS MOLINA

Carlos Molina moved to the United States in 1985 after earning a degree in economics and business in his native Ecuador. He began working for the Bellini shoe company as an accountant but shifted to product development. From 1992 he worked as a salesman and line builder at Coup d'Etat. After seven years he was ready to start his own line and opened Molina Inc., producing high-fashion footwear.

CASADEI

Manufacturer founded in 1958 by Quinto and Flora Casadei in Cesena, Italy. By 1964 the company was already exporting high-fashion quality footwear and under the direction of the founders' son Cesare Casadei, 70 per cent of its footwear now goes for export.

CASADEI
Advertisement for Casadei, Spring 1986

CASADEI
Black patent leather D'Orsay pumps with straps, late 1970s

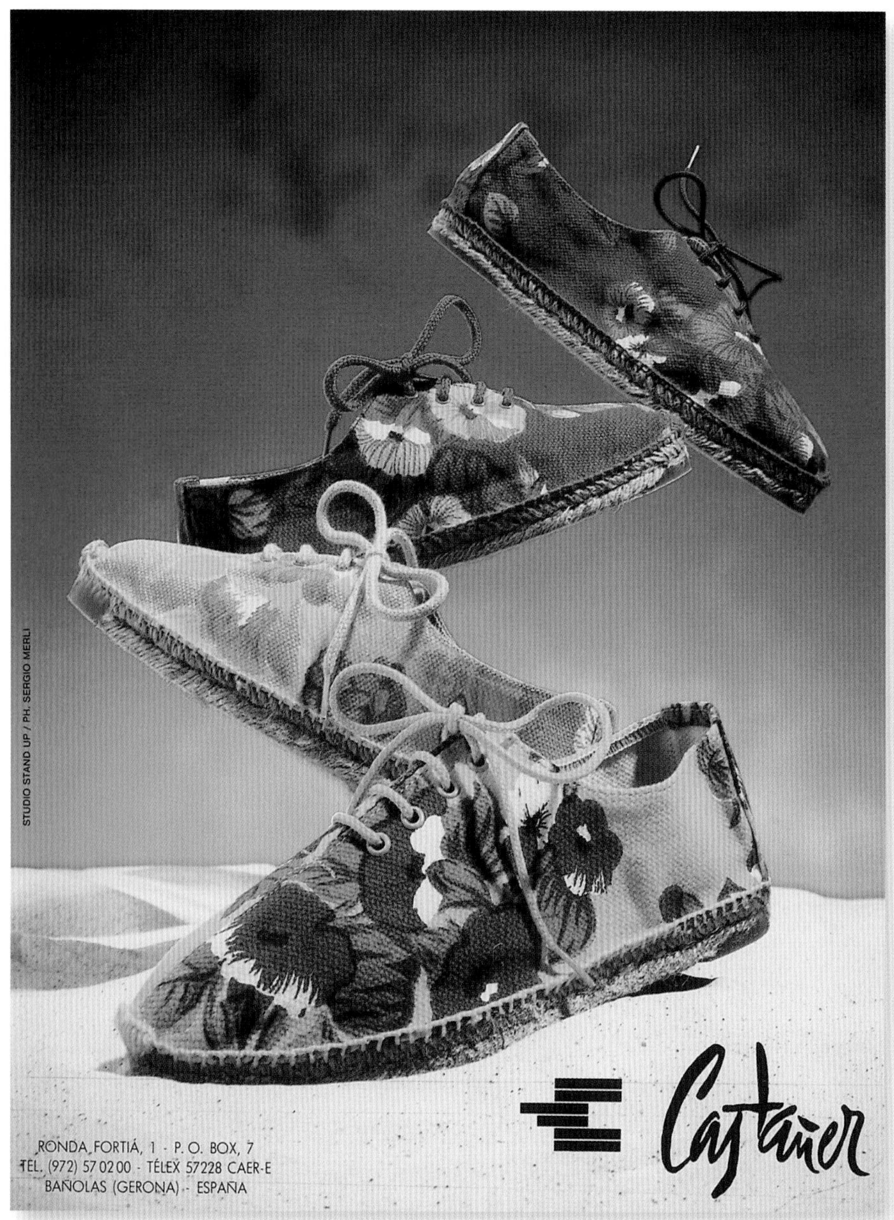

STUDIO STAND UP / PH. SERGIO MERLI
Castañer
RONDA FORTIÁ, 1 - P. O. BOX, 7
TEL. (972) 57 02 00 - TÉLEX 57228 CAER-E
BAÑOLAS (GERONA) - ESPAÑA

CASTAÑER

Advertisement for Castañer, Spring 1986

CASTAÑER
Castañer wedge-heeled espadrilles for Yves Saint Laurent, mid-1970s

CASTAÑER

Luis Castañer founded a small workshop producing *alpargatos* (espadrilles) in 1927. Although the company was nationalized in 1936 to produce military footwear, the company continued under family management. In the early 1970s Lorenzo and Isabel Castañer attended a fair in Paris where Yves Saint Laurent discovered their shoes and commissioned them to create wedge-heeled versions for his label. Although Castañer has expanded into making leather shoes and boots under its own brand name, its wedge-heeled espadrilles have also been made for the Louis Vuitton and **CHRISTIAN LOUBOUTIN** labels.

CELS ENTERPRISES

This women's footwear company was founded in 1971 by Robert and Carol Goldman and is headquartered in Los Angeles. Originally a manufacturer selling to mass merchants, the company has developed eight branded divisions. Creative International, formed in 1971, focuses on private-label business for volume retailers. Chinese Laundry (1981) is the high-fashion line. On Your Feet (1985) is aimed at a younger, more casual customer. CL by Laundry is a value-based brand. Dirty Laundry is made for the urban street-smart customer. CL Wash was launched for sporty, active women. Little Laundry, launched in 2004, is made for girls. The most recent addition, Vintage Laundry, was launched in 2008 and features shoes based on vintage styles.

CESARE PACIOTTI

Giuseppe Paciotti founded a shoe factory in Civitanova Marche, Italy, in 1948 to produce a line of men's hand-finished footwear under the brand name Paris. His son, Cesare Paciotti, studied art in Bologna and then travelled the world, before taking over his parents' business in 1980. He began producing shoes for Gianni Versace, Roberto Cavalli, Romeo Gigli and Dolce & Gabbana. In 1990 Paciotti expanded its previously small line of women's high-fashion footwear and now produces two main lines, Cesare Paciotti, and Paciotti 4US, a younger market brand.

CESARE PACIOTTI
Advertisement for Cesare Paciotti, Autumn 1995

CHARLES DAVID

Charles Malka opened his first shoe boutique in Hollywood in 1988 under the store name Charles David. The family-owned business controls all aspects of its shoe brand, from design and distribution to marketing and retail operations. The company has expanded to twenty-five retail stores across the US as well as through fashion boutiques and department stores where it sells shoes, and now handbags, under the labels 'Charles David', and 'Charles' by Charles David.

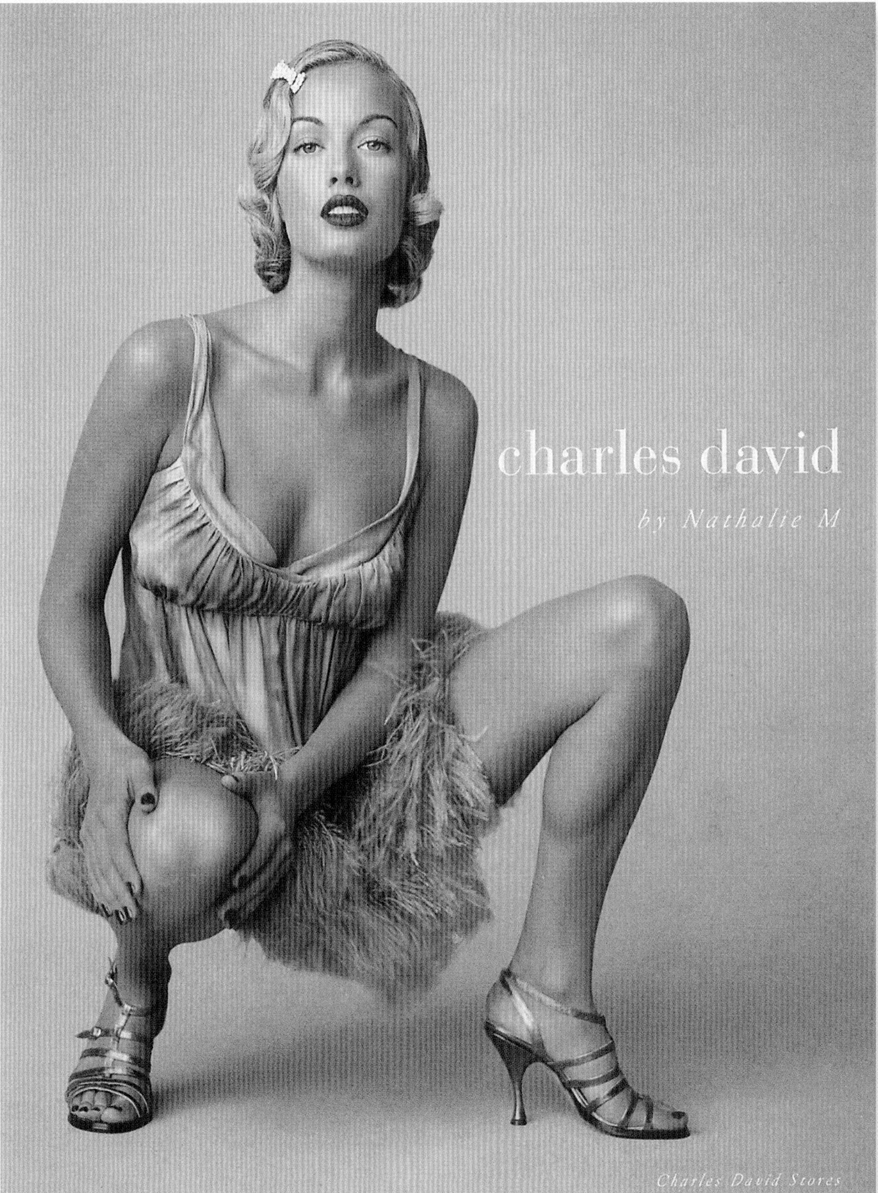

CHARLES DAVID
Advertisement for Charles David,
Spring 1995

CHARLES JOURDAN

Charles Jourdan (1883–1976) worked his way up through the shoe industry in Romans, France, from a small workshop in 1921 (some sources say 1919), to a larger factory and the launch of a prêt-à-porter line in 1928. His sons joined the family business during the Second World War when, like most French companies, Jourdan was making shoes in substitute materials because of leather shortages. In the post-war years Jourdan's son Roland used the company's reputation for chic elegance to expand into the British and American markets. In 1953 he made an arrangement with American shoe retailer **GENESCO** that Charles Jourdan would be the only French factory to export shoes to the US. In 1957 Charles's three sons took over the business, which by then had a reputation for quality ready-to-wear footwear, and opened a boutique at 5 boulevard de la Madeleine in Paris. In 1959 the company was granted a licence to manufacture **ROGER VIVIER'S** shoe designs for the house of Dior. Charles Jourdan was very successful in the 1960s and 1970s, opening shoe boutiques around the world and designing lines for several prêt-à-porter collections, including Pierre Cardin. Roland Jourdan received a Neiman Marcus Award for distinguished service in the field of fashion in 1968, just as Charles Jourdan shoes were becoming internationally known high-fashion footwear. The company expanded, perhaps too rapidly, and in 1981 Roland stepped down and Jourdan ceased to be a family-run business. In the early 1990s Charles Jourdan was making shoes under its own labels, Charles Jourdan and Seducta, as well as for CJ Bis, Karl Lagerfeld and Enrico Coveri. The early 1990s recession took its toll on the company, which had to pull back from many of its retail stores and focus on restructuring. In 2009 Charles Jourdan, now owned by Groupe Royer, staged an aggressive comeback at Paris Fashion Week with new collections by designer **ALEXANDRA NEEL**.

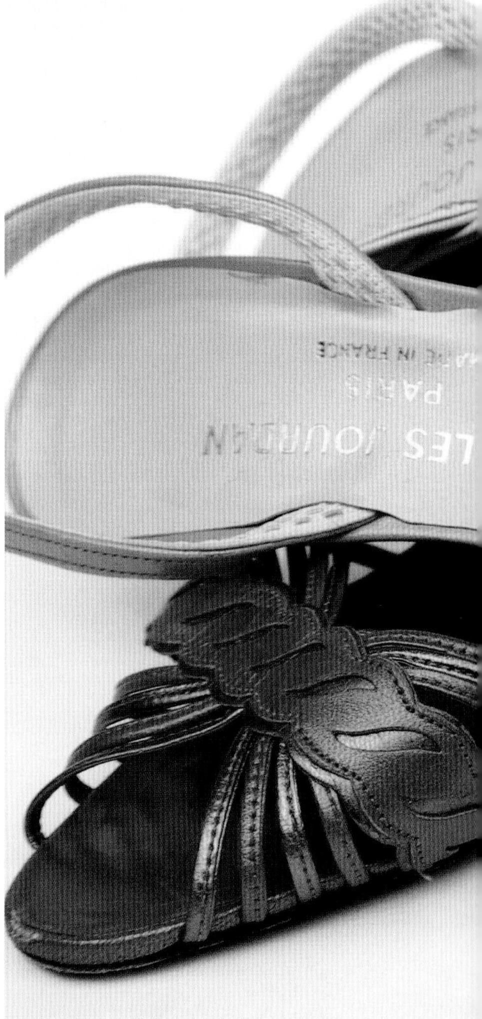

CHARLES JOURDAN
Kid and snakeskin sandals in a variety of colours, 1983

CHELSEA COBBLER
Purple leather button boots with appliqués of silver moons and yellow stars and suns, 1968

CHELSEA COBBLER

Established in 1967 on King's Road, London, by the designers Richard Smith and Mandy Wilkins, Chelsea Cobbler created bespoke shoes for clients as well as an exuberant ready-to-wear line. By the mid-1970s their shoes, which included imports, were becoming more mainstream to appeal to a larger audience. They also expanded the number of locations, including a shop within Harrods.

CHIE MIHARA

Born in Porto Alegre, Brazil, in 1968, of Japanese parents, Chie Mihara studied fashion design in Japan and New York. She has worked as a designer for **SAM & LIBBY** and **CHARLES JOURDAN**, and in 2001 she launched her own line of footwear. Her shoes have been called romantic, comfortable, sculptural and beautiful.

CHIKOSHOES

Manufacturer founded in 1999 in Shanghai, China, by Judy Chin and Rumbert Kolkman. Chickoshoes makes a wide variety of shoes, from high-fashion to sportswear, working to designs supplied by its clients.

CHIKOSHOES
Black D'Orsay pump, 2009

CHINESE LAUNDRY *see* CELS ENTERPRISES

CHRISTIAN LOUBOUTIN

Born in 1963, Louboutin trained at **CHARLES JOURDAN** and sold freelance designs to Chanel, Yves Saint Laurent and **ROGER VIVIER** before launching his own label. In 1991 he opened his own shop at the Passage Véro-Dodat in Paris. Louboutin describes himself as a shoe fetishist and says that early in his career he was inspired by cabaret showgirls to design flashy stage shoes. The most sensuous part of a woman's foot, according to Louboutin, is the inside curve of the arch. The soles of Christian Louboutin shoes are painted with bright red lacquer, regardless of their upper colour, and the top lifts of his heels are sometimes shaped to leave rosette imprints. He calls these his 'Follow Me' shoes.

CHRISTIAN LOUBOUTIN
Above left: 'Rodita' white canvas and leather platform sandals with zippers, adjustable crisscross straps, leather-covered ankle buckles and Louboutin's signature red sole, 2009

Above: 'Very Croise' double-platform sling-back sandals in white leather with silver metallic details, peep toe and Louboutin's signature red sole, 2009

CLARK, MARGARET *see* **MARGARET JERROLD**

CLARKS

A family shoemaking business that began in the 1820s as C. & J. Clarks became one of England's largest manufacturers of the twentieth century. Clarks sold the brands Torbrand and Hygienic before launching its own-brand shoe in 1920. In 1949 Nathan Clark designed a crêpe-soled suede boot he called the Desert Boot. Clark took the idea from the English army officer's regulation boots he had seen while in service in North Africa during the Second World War. The style was a huge seller for the company by the late 1950s and set a precedent for men's leisure shoes. Another winning style followed in 1966, called the Wallabee. In the 1980s the family-held firm encountered financial troubles. After 1996 the problems became so dire the company moved its production to Brazil and India. Clarks attempted to re-situate itself in 2001 with the acquisition of the German manufacturer Elefanten, but by 2005 the last of the British production facilities were permanently closed. Clarks produces several brand-name lines including Indigo (fashion forward), Privo (youthful active casual wear) and Bostonian (men's dress shoes).

CLARKS
Advertisement for Clarks, Spring 1963

CLONE *see* **BORDESE, BRUNO**

COLE HAAN

Trafton Cole and Eddie Haan introduced the first Cole Haan shoe, a man's oxford, in Chicago in 1928. By the 1950s the company had become known for its collegiate styles for young men, including saddle shoes, white bucks and penny loafers. In 1979 the company began a line of women's footwear. In the 1980s it promoted dressy casuals, including boat shoes and driving moccasins. From 1984 it led the so-called 'brown shoe' market with athletic-inspired natural-coloured leather sport shoes. Nike acquired Cole Haan in 1988 but the company retained its name. In 1999 Cole Haan issued shoes inspired by its patterns from the twenties and thirties. From 2006 Cole Haan's dress shoes for women offered Nike air-sole technology for comfort.

COLE·HAAN

fine footwear and accessories. for men, women and children.

the *corinna* sling-back. in natural or black linen with a rust croc toe.

the *vanessa* mule. in natural or black linen with rust lizard trim.

For stores near you write: Cole-Haan Dept. R3 North Elm St. Yarmouth, ME 04096-5002

COLE HAAN
Advertisement for Cole Haan, Spring 1994

COLLECTIVE BRANDS

Collective Brands was formed in 2007, when Payless Shoes bought out Stride Rite and Collective Licensing International, two companies which had themselves grown by amalgamation. Stride Rite had been established in 1919 as a children's shoe line, and Collective Licensing had brought together Airwalk and American Eagle, among others. Collective Brands Inc. is now the largest non-athletic shoe company in the western hemisphere. It operates retail stores and manufactures a wide range of brands, including Abaete, Airwalk, American Eagle, Champion, Dexter, Disney, Grasshoppers, Hannah Montana, Keds, Lela Rose, Patricia Field, Saucony, Sims, Skate Attack, Stride Rite, Sperry Top-Sider, Tommy Hilfiger footwear, Ultra-Wheels and Vision Street Wear.

CONSOLIDATED SHOE
Advertisement for the brand Off The Beaten Track by Consolidated Shoe, 2009

CONSOLIDATED SHOE

Right Advertisement for Irregular Choice by Consolidated Shoe, 2009

Below Advertisement for Poetic Licence and Irregular Choice by Consolidated Shoe, 2009

CONSOLIDATED SHOE

Founded in 1898 as Lynchburg Shoe in Lynchburg, Virginia, the company changed its name as it acquired other manufacturers. Today the company makes or imports shoes under the labels **APEPAZZA**, Nicole, Madeline, **IRREGULAR CHOICE** and Poetic Licence and, since 2008, Off The Beaten Track, designed for travellers. Since 2008 it has discontinued its labels Ipanema and Palladium. Its Nicole brand is designed by Maurizio Celin, who studied advertising design at Padua and shoe design in nearby Stra. He became a designer for various companies, including **NINE WEST**, **SERGIO ROSSI** and Enzo **ANGIOLINI**, before setting up his own studio in 1985.

CRADDOCK-TERRY SHOE CORPORATION
Left Advertisement for Natural Bridge brand shoes by Craddock-Terry, Spring 1950

Below Advertisement for Auditions brand shoes by Craddock-Terry, Spring 1968

COUROMODA

Couromoda began in the early 1970s and has grown to become the leading representative of the Brazilian shoe industry, through its trade fairs and promotions for foreign markets. The 1,200 exhibitors that showed at the January 2009 Couromoda fair in São Paulo, Brazil, represented more than 3,000 brands, 90 per cent of Brazilian shoe production.

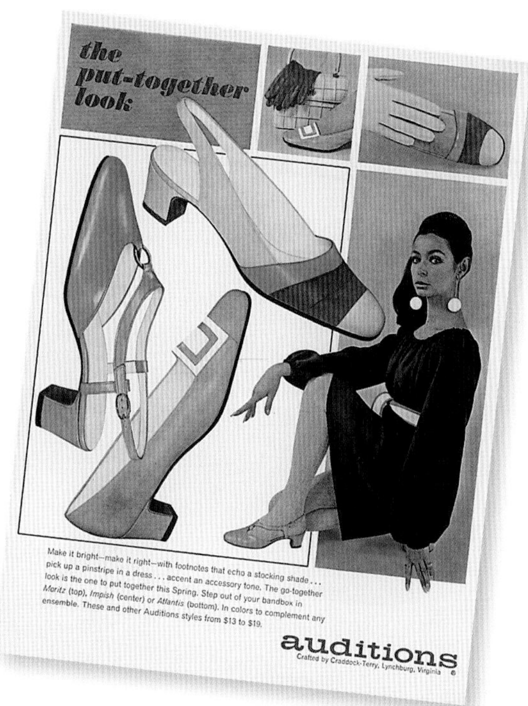

CRADDOCK-TERRY SHOE CORPORATION

Founded in 1888 in Lynchburg, Virginia, the Craddock-Terry Shoe Corporation was best known for its line of women's shoes, especially under the Auditions label in the 1960s. The company filed for bankruptcy protection in 1987, just shy of its 100th anniversary. A government contract to make shoes for the armed forces revitalized the company under the new name Craddock-Terry Inc.

CROCS

A waterproof, bacteria-resistant ethylene vinyl acetate foam resin called croslite™ was patented in 1998. The lightweight, non-marking, slip- and odour-resistant material was made into an injection-moulded clog by a Canadian company for use in day spas. An example of the black day-spa clogs came to the attention of George Boedecker Jr., owner of the American company Western Brands. Boedecker's partner Scott Seamans altered the style to include a back strap, and in 2002 they were launched as boating shoes under the name Crocs. Crocs became a massive fashion hit in summer 2006, and their success spawned imitation 'Crock-Offs'. The company tightened its trademarks but since 2007 the company has seen a severe decline in its sales.

CYDWOQ

Descended from a long line of Armenian shoemakers, Rafi Balouzian began as a clothing designer in Los Angeles before founding his shoe company, CYDWOQ, in Burbank, California, in 1996. The company produces durable fashion footwear designed for walking comfort, using eco-conscious vegetable-tanned leathers, in as few pieces as possible, and organic glues.

CROCS
'Cayman' clogs with ankle strap in Croc's exclusive croslite™ material, *c.* 2006–10

DANIBLACK *see* **SCHWARTZ & BENJAMIN**

DANIELE TUCCI

Italian company founded in Milan in 1984 specializing in woven leather shoes and sandals.

DAN POST BOOT COMPANY

Dan Post was founded in the mid-1960s in Tennessee, when the trend for western-style boots was on the rise. The brands Laredo and Dingo were added in the 1970s.

DANSKO

Founded in 1990 by Peter Kiellerup and Mandy Cabot, Dansko literally means 'Danish Shoe'. The company is known for heavy-soled clog-style slip-on shoes with two-piece uppers.

DAN POST BOOT COMPANY
Advertisement for Dan Post boots, Autumn/Winter 1992

DANSKO
Clog with rocker bottom, 2009

DAVID WYATT
'Plumage' red pump, 2009

DAVID WYATT

David Wyatt began as a designer of women's fashions before turning his attention to women's shoes in 2002. His collections tend towards baroque femininity with abundant uses of rich textiles and needlework.

DEB SHOE COMPANY *see* **WOLFF SHOE COMPANY**

DECKERS

In Santa Barbara, California, in 1973 surfing enthusiast Doug Otto began producing nylon and rubber sandals under the brand name Driftwood Dan. Hawaiians apparently called the flip-flop sandals 'Deckas', slang for the soles that resembled the layers of decks on a cruise ship, and Otto took over the name for his product in 1975. In 1985 Deckers entered into a licensing agreement to produce and distribute Teva sandals, developed by Mark Thatcher in 1984, and in 2002 it took over the company. In 1993 Deckers acquired **SIMPLE SHOES**, a company created in 1991 by Eric Meyer that manufactured an athletic, casual style of footwear. The same year the company became Deckers Outdoor Corporation and shortly afterwards the original Deckers brand was suspended in favour of the development of Simple Shoes and Teva; the brand was reintroduced in June 2008. In 1995 Deckers bought **UGG HOLDINGS**, founded in 1979 by Brian Smith to import sheepskin boots from Australia to the United States.

DELMAN *see* **HERMAN DELMAN**

DE ROBERT

Italian company founded in 1955 which produces women's comfortable fashion shoes under the brand names De Robert (youthful styles), Zenob (comfort styles) and Fly. The shoes are sold through high-end retailers around the world.

DIANA FERRARI

Located in Richmond, Victoria, since 1979, Diana Ferrari has grown to become a leading Australian shoe manufacturer. In 1983 the company launched a comfort line under the name Supersoft and in 2000 opened its first retail store, also selling apparel and accessories.

DIEGO DELLA VALLE
Metallic finish kid sandals, late 1970s

DIEGO DELLA VALLE

Della Valle was born in 1954, the third generation of Italian shoe designers and manufacturers. He emerged in the late 1970s as a designer of quality shoes and has since designed for Versace, Ferre, Lagerfeld, Fendi, Krizia, Lacroix, Beene, Azzedine Alaïa, Gigli and Calvin Klein. His first Tod boutique of luxury casuals opened in 1979. He introduced the driving moccasin in 1988 and expanded Tod's to include bags and accessories in 1997. He acquired **ROGER VIVIER** in the mid- 1990s.

DIEGO DOLCINI

Dolcini was born in Naples and trained in Milan. He started as an architecture student, like many shoe designers, but switched before the end of his course. He launched his own line of shoes in 1994 and collaborated with several leading brands, including **BRUNO MAGLI** and Pucci. Between 2001 and 2004 he was creative director of footwear at **GUCCI**.

DI SANDRO *see* MAGLI, SANDRO

DOC MARTENS

Suffering discomfort following a skiing accident in 1945, Dr Klaus Maertens, a German orthopaedic doctor, designed a shoe with an air-cushioned sole. In collaboration with a colleague, Dr Herbert Funck, he perfected and patented the resulting design, and marketed the shoes in Germany. Looking for a larger manufacturer and distributor, Maertens connected with the family-owned British manufacturer R. Griggs, which was awarded the global licence in 1959. Griggs used the sole on an industrial-style boot, but altered it from rubber to PVC to make it more stain-resistant, and added stitching in contrasting colours to the uppers. The inventor's name was anglicized to Dr. Martens, popularized as Doc Martens. The original boot design was known as 1460, that is 1 April 1960, the date the first pair was made. They were marketed as industry and workwear, and the first steady customers were the British police, postal workers and labourers. In the late 1970s the boots were picked up as aggressive-looking but comfortable streetwear by punks and skinheads, and sales rocketed. In the 1980s the company extended control over the market by buying up the licences of other makers of Dr. Martens and expanding the choice of styles and colours. The boots acquired a range of associations: neo-nazi skinheads wore them, complete with symbolic white laces, but they were ordered also by the Vatican. By the early 1990s, the patented sole was found everywhere: **MANOLO BLAHNÍK** fashioned high-style couture shoes from them. Although the sole was patented, other elements of the brand were not, and the 1990s saw many copies drive down Griggs' own sales. It responded by buying the American distributor AirWair and tightening control of the brand through litigation against imitators, claiming that Doc Martens are not just a brand but a lifestyle. Facing serious losses, the company moved production to China in 2003.

DOC MARTENS
Black and red boots with sickle appliqués, mid-1990s

DOMINICI

Manufacturer founded in 1980 by Alvaro Dominici that creates high-fashion footwear for shops in Italy, Austria, Greece, Israel, Germany and Denmark.

Dr Martens

DONALD J. PLINER

Born in 1943, Pliner grew up in the shoe business, beginning with an apprenticeship at his father's **FLORSHEIM** shoe store. He struck out on his own in 1967 and by 1974 was operating the Right Bank Shoe Company in Beverly Hills, which specialized in new designers like **MAUD FRIZON** and **STEPHANE KÉLIAN**. Pliner also produced shoes for his store and created an eponymous line of women's shoes in 1989, followed by a men's line in 1998. The Italian-made shoes are sold primarily in the United States. Approximately one million pairs of shoes were made under the Donald J. Pliner label in 2009.

DR. SCHOLL

Born in 1882, William Mathias Scholl apprenticed as a shoe repairer and worked as a shoe sales clerk, where he became familiar with common foot ailments. He earned a medical degree from the Illinois Medical College, now Loyola University, and in 1907 started the Scholl Manufacturing Co. to create footcare products, including an arch support called the Foot-eazer. Scholl founded the Illinois College of Chiropody and Orthopaedics in 1912. In 1958 the first Scholl Exercise sandal was created, consisting of a wooden sole with a raised toe crest, requiring the wearer's toes to grip the sole of the sandal. Scholl died in 1968, leaving the company under the direction of his two nephews, who took it public in 1971. The following year, the exercise sandal went from medical use to international fashion hit, with over a million pairs being sold in the United States alone. Exercise sandals enjoyed a revival in the early 1990s and the wooden sandals even appeared in runway shows by fashion designers Michael Kors and Isaac Mizrahi. Dr. Scholl products are now made in China and imported by the **BROWN SHOE COMPANY** into the United States.

Shoes off. Scholls on.

DONALD J. PLINER
Advertisement for Donald J. Pliner, Autumn 2006

DR. SCHOLL
Advertisement for Dr. Scholl, Autumn 1976

DUNN & MCCARTHY

John Dunn founded the Dunn & McCarthy Shoe Company in 1867 in Auburn, New York. The original labour force came from the nearby Auburn Correctional Facility. The company specialized in comfort-fitting fashion footwear. Its brand Enna Jetticks was introduced by 1930, and its walking shoes, Hill and Dale, followed a couple of years later. Its shoes followed the leading fashions, but not to the extreme, always providing stylish shoes where comfort was considered first. Dunn & McCarthy filed for bankruptcy in October 1989 and closed in March 1990.

fresh from Hill and Dale
Caprice: one of the new crop-heeled, high-spirited Hill and Dales springing up right now in all the nicest stores in town. From $20.
Dixon-Bartlett, Inc., 2413 Eastern Ave., Baltimore, Md. 21224

DUNN & MCCARTHY
Advertisement for Hill and Dale brand shoes by Dunn & McCarthy, Spring 1966

EARTH SHOES

Anne Kalso was born in Denmark and worked as a yoga instructor. She observed how, when walking on the beach, the heel sinks into the sand, similar to the yoga 'mountain pose'. Feeling this stance must have health benefits, Kalso tested designs for shoes with lowered or 'negative' heels. In 1968 she opened a store in Copenhagen to sell her Kalso Minus Heel shoe. The following year, vacationing Americans Raymond and Eleanor Jacobs discovered the store and entered into an agreement with Kalso to distribute the shoes in the US. The store opened on East 17th Street in New York on 1 April 1970, which happened to be the first internationally observed Earth Day, so Eleanor Jacobs put a sign in the window advertising the product as Earth Shoes. The first factory in America making Earth Shoes opened in September 1972. By 1974 advertising campaigns and widespread press coverage made demand for the shoes skyrocket. The American company's inability to supply its franchise stores led to its dissolution in 1977. By 2000 the brand was revitalized in the US under a new partnership with Kalso by Meynard Designs, and sold through a website. The shoes were reintroduced to the marketplace in 2001. For the 40th anniversary of Earth Day in April 2010, Earth Shoes introduced a biodegradable sole called BioStep.

ECCO

Left **'Vermont' tall zip boot in brown leather, 2009**

Below **'Bouillion' ballerina flat in purple suede, 2009**

Bottom **'Lite' flat in black leather, 2009**

EASTLAND
Right **Brown leather moccasin construction shoes, 2009**

ECCO
Below **'Also Soft' shoes in black leather and croc-patterned patent leather, 2009**

EASTLAND

This family-owned business in Freeport, Maine, was founded in 1955 and produces casual 'brown market' slip-ons, sandals, mary-janes and classic boot styles. Eastland manufactures under the brand Eastland, as well as Underfoot and Southwest Moccasin Co.

ECCO

Founded in 1963 by Birte and Karl Toosbuy in Bredebro, Denmark, Ecco footwear strives for a blend of design and podiatric technology. Echo uses direct-injection moulded soles, which are flexible, durable and supportive. Their first big seller was called Joke, launched in 1978. Karl's daughter, Hanni Toosbuy Kasprzak, took over the company after his death in 2004.

ECO-DRAGON

Founded in 1993 by Eric and Wes Crain. Its fair-trade, eco-friendly hemp shoes are made in China near Xi-an, where 7,000 life-sized terracotta soldiers of emperor Qin Shi Huang were buried wearing similar hemp-soled footwear.

EDER

Manufacturer founded in Italy in 1983 by Mauro De Bari, producing casual and leisure sandals. Its principle market is Italy but it is expanding abroad.

EDISON BROTHERS STORES

Henry, Mark, Irving and Simon Edison began Chandler's shoe store in Atlanta, Georgia, in 1922, and eventually became the largest shoe-store owners in the United States, with over 5,000 shops. Chandler's first became famous in the 1920s as every pair of shoes was priced at \$6. The brothers specialized in fancy fashion styles, shoe 'millinery', and exploited economies of scale to keep down prices. In 1923 the first of many Baker's shoe stores was opened to sell a more affordable

EDISON BROTHERS STORES
Left Advertisement for Chandlers, a chain of stores owned by Edison Brothers, December 1971

Below Advertisement for Chandlers, a chain of stores owned by Edison Brothers, Autumn 1958

Harper's Bazaar
Ready for it?
Are your vibes right for a high wrapped rocker sole, suede strapped, lifted on a 3½ inch heel? Do your juices jump for yellow, hot pink, purple, turquoise suede on white kid; white or beige on brown, black on black? Yes? Then come to Chandlers. Colors: 695 Fifth Ave., N.Y. and Florida stores. Black in all stores. 16.99
CHANDLERS
big looks for little!

For evening splendor, the tiara shoe... high-heeled satin sheath featuring a sun-burst of rhinestones at the toe. This French Room Originals design comes in black, red, green, jonquil and hyacinth; available at Chandler's Fifth Avenue and at Chandler's salons across the nation. A DIVISION OF EDISON BROTHERS STORES INC.
French Room Originals
CHANDLER'S
SHOE SALONS

line of footwear. There was already a store of that name in California, so the store west of the Rockies was known as Leed's. During the Depression a chain to sell even cheaper shoes was launched under the name Burt's. By 1948 Edison Brothers Inc. had 200 stores across the country, including its first store in a shopping mall. By the time the company was running 1,000 stores, in 1973, the children of the original brothers were operating the company and were diversifying its interests, acquiring clothing and accessory stores. In Houston and Tucson in 1972 Edison Brothers opened its first store aimed at the youth market, called Wild Pair, which specialized in unisex styles. By the mid-1970s the Chandler's stores were feeling the competition from imports, although the budget-conscious Baker's, Leed's and Burt's continued to open in the proliferating shopping malls. This led to market saturation and declining profitability in the 1980s. However, growth has continued for the company through acquisitions of non-shoe businesses, primarily clothing, but also restaurants and entertainment facilities such as video arcades.

EDMUNDO CASTILLO

Born in Puerto Rico in 1967, Castillo moved to New York to learn shoemaking. Eight years of training at Donna Karan led to a brief stint at Polo Ralph Lauren before he returned to Donna Karan to design the Donna Karan and DKNY men's lines. In 2001 Castillo won the Perry Ellis award for his new signature line of shoes. In 2006 he became the designer at **SERGIO ROSSI**.

EDUARD RHEINBERGER

Manufacturer founded in 1882 in Pirmasens, Germany. A large modern factory was built in 1906 and by 1913 one million pairs of shoes a year were being made. By 1962 production had increased to 1.5 million pairs, but the company went into decline in the late 1960s and was bought out by Rudolf Seibel in 1973.

EDWARD AND HOLMES *see* HOLMES OF NORWICH

EGBERT VAN DER DOES

Dutch-born Egbert van der Does worked as an artist for twenty-three years before combining his artistic talents with the technical skills of shoemaking that he learned from a course at a vocational institute. His made-to-order shoes for men and women are known for their unusual, contemporary combinations of materials, colours and styles.

EGBERT VAN DER DOES
Above and opposite **Laced shoes with closed and open uppers in a variety of materials and colours, designed and made by Egbert van der Does, 2006–9**

EJECT
Advertisement for Eject, Autumn/Winter 2009

EJECT

Portuguese shoe brand launched in 2001 for the urban youth fashion market. Sold throughout Europe, Canada and New Zealand.

ELATA

Manufacturer founded in 1923 by Salvatore Nicolazzo in Casarano, Italy. Nicolazzo's was one of the first factories in Italy to use assembly-line production methods. Salvatore died in 1959 but the company continued under family ownership. The company was incorporated in 1979. Elata produces high-fashion women's footwear.

ELIZA DI VENEZIA

Founded in 1980, this Italian company now produces high-fashion forward styles for young women for the European, Russian and American markets.

EL VAQUERO

Gaetano Bonifacio imported Italian-made footwear into the United States under the label El Vaquero. The shoes were sold through about 150 retailers during the 1980s, primarily in New York and Los Angeles, but also through the Neiman Marcus department store. Bonifacio was partners in the company with his wife from 1981 to 1989, but following their divorce he discontinued operations. The brand was revived in 1992.

EL VAQUERO

Above **Advertisement for El Vaquero, Spring 1985**

Right **Leather and cotton net sandal-boots decorated with rhinestone-studded brass stars, *c.* 1985**

EMMA HOPE

Trained at London's Cordwainers College, English-born Hope produced her first collection in 1984. The first of her three shops in London opened in 1987, and in 2003 she opened another in Tokyo. Hope's shoes are made in Italy and often show influence from historical styles. She has designed shoe lines for Paul Smith and Anna Sui.

ENCORE SHOE CORPORATION

Earl Katz founded Encore in Rochester, New Hampshire, in 1963 to make espadrilles under the label Pappagallos. The company's chief designer, Al Charette, introduced the fashion-forward Zodiac label to appeal to cost-conscious twenty-somethings through venues like Bloomingdale's. Zodiac was a leading manufacturer of trendy footwear throughout the 1970s but in the early 1980s sales and profits began to shrink and the company began to rely on imports. Encore tried, unsuccessfully, to create an athletic line of Zodiac footwear but the family-owned business was bought out in 1992 and the original factory was closed.

EMMA HOPE
Emma Hope patterned pumps, 1988

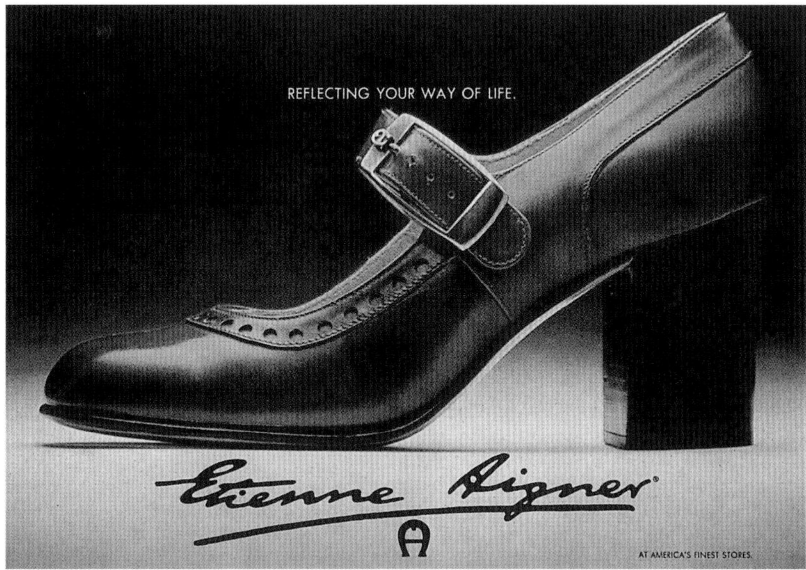

ETIENNE AIGNER
Advertisement for Etienne Aigner, Autumn 1969

ENNA JETTICKS *see* DUNN & MCCARTHY

ENZELLA

Enzella was founded in 1969 in Tuscany as a manufacturer of women's footwear for export. As the quality of its footwear improved, two brands developed: Enzodisiena, classic fashion footwear, and Tinta Unita, younger, fashion-forward styles.

ETIENNE AIGNER

Hungarian-born Etienne Aigner learned bookbinding when he moved to Paris in 1926 at the age of twenty-two. After emigrating to the United States in 1949 he began making belts, often in burgundy leather, which became his signature colour. In 1959 he opened his first shop, which carried leather accessories, but he soon began to make sandals and by the late 1960s he was also making classic style shoes for the established woman.

EVINS, DAVID
Opposite **Brocade sling-back shoes covered with topaz rhinestones, with a painted sole, *c.* 1958**

Below **Black lurex shot textile cocktail ankle boots, *c.* 1960**

EVINS, DAVID

Evins was born in England in 1909, and moved with his family to the United States at the age of thirteen. After studying illustration at the Pratt Institute in New York, he worked on *Vogue*, but he was fired after **HERMAN DELMAN** objected to the artistic licence Evins took with his shoes. Delman told Evins, 'Get yourself a job as a designer if you want to be one.' He went to work as a pattern-maker and opened his own studio. His work was interrupted by his service in the Second World War, but when it ended he and his brother Lee re-opened the studio, Evins Inc., in New York and started designing in conjunction with **I. MILLER** on whose label his name appeared. In 1949 he received both a Neiman Marcus Award and a Coty Award for his contribution to shoe design. As a bespoke shoemaker he made shoes for first ladies, royalty and film stars, including Claudette Colbert and Elizabeth Taylor, for their respective roles as Cleopatra in 1934 and 1963. In the late 1950s he entered into a partnership with **MARIO VALENTINO** in Italy, and during his life designed shoes for Mainbocher, Valentina, Charles James, Galanos, Norell, Balenciaga, Calvin Klein, Bill Blass, Ralph Lauren, Oscar de la Renta and Geoffrey Beene. In 1968 he sold his business to retail giant **GENESCO** but continued to design and oversee production of Evins footwear. In 1975 the **UNITED STATES SHOE CORPORATION** acquired the Evins division and he remained actively involved in the design and production of his shoes until the year before his death in 1991.

FAMOLARE, JOE

Born in 1932, Joe Famolare was twelve when he began working at his father's pattern and last company. After studying musical theatre, Famolare worked for **CAPEZIO** in the early 1960s. From 1965 to 1968 he worked for the **UNITED STATES SHOE CORPORATION** on its Bandolino brand, but in 1969 he turned entrepreneur and founded Famolare Inc. In 1973 he received a Coty award for a moulded rubber clog, and this success was followed by a comfort walking shoe with a wavy-bottomed thick rubber sole called Get There. The shoe, which featured a bicycle as its logo, became an explosive hit in 1975, but the Hi There shoe, with a three-inch heel, failed to capture the same interest a couple of years later. Get There lost ground to illicit copies, and in the 1980s the market for trainers usurped comfort shoes. In 1987 Famolare licensed his name to the United States Shoe Corporation.

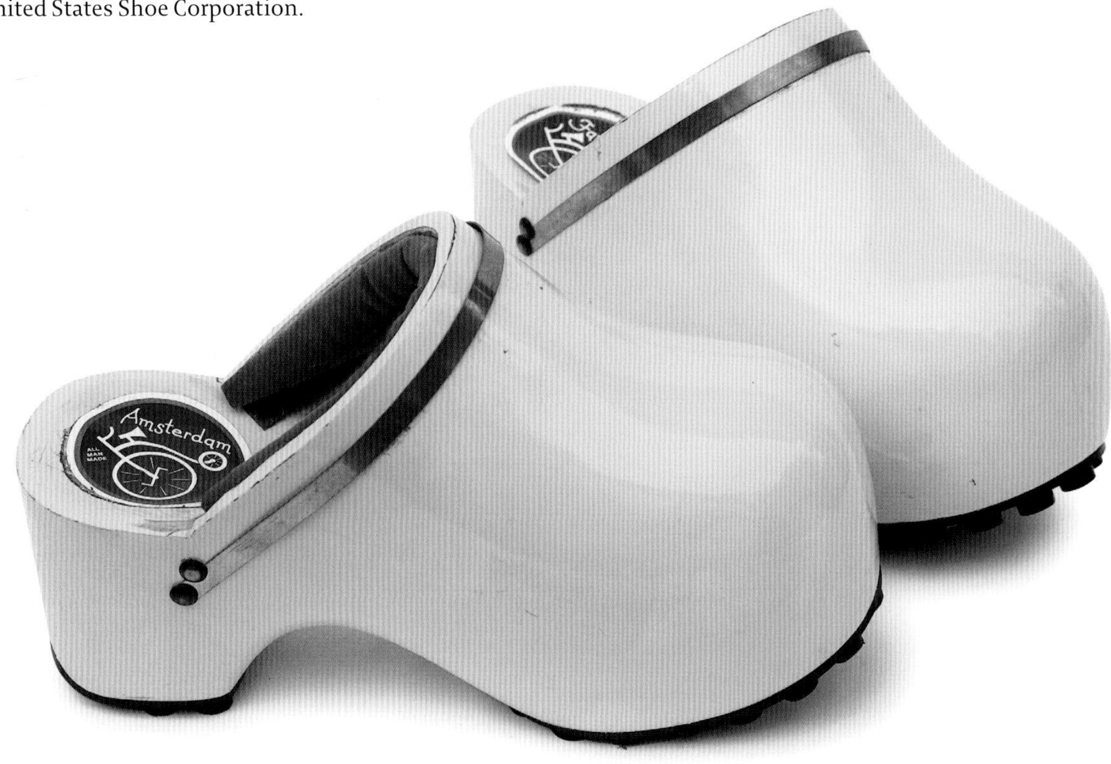

FAMOLARE, JOE
Yellow plastic moulded clogs, 1974

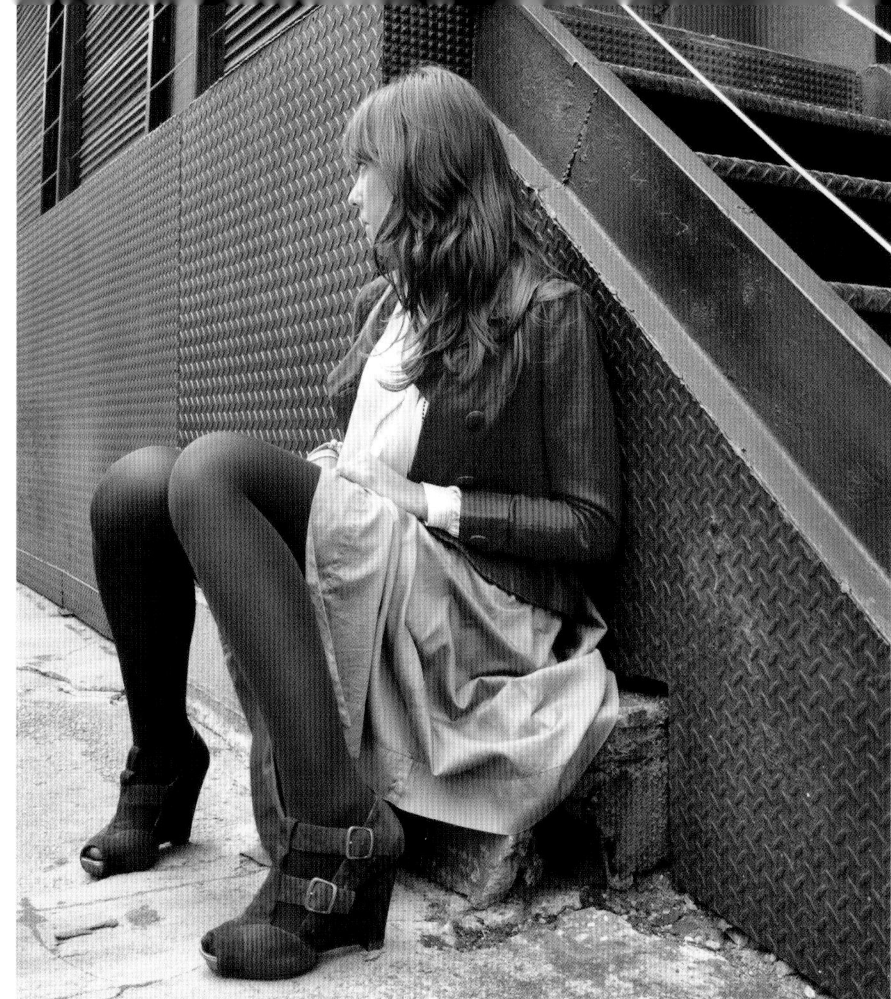

FARYLROBIN FOOTWEAR
Advertisement for Farylrobin, Autumn 2009

FARYLROBIN FOOTWEAR

Founded by Faryl Robin Morse in New York in 2002, the youth-orientated shoe company produces seasonal basics following high-fashion trends, but markets them primarily online instead of in print ads. About 25 per cent of sales are directly through the internet.

FERRAGAMO *see* SALVATORE FERRAGAMO

FIAMMA FERRAGAMO

Fiamma Ferragamo (1941–98) was the eldest child of shoemaker **SALVATORE FERRAGAMO**. She began working for her father at the age of sixteen and took on a leading role when he died in 1960. In 1967 she launched her most successful shoe design, a round-toed low-heeled pump with grosgrain ribbon trim. The Vara became, and remains, an iconic modern classic, for which Fiamma received the Neiman Marcus Award for Distinguished Service. She was responsible for designing Ferragamo shoes for almost forty years, and was influential in transforming her father's company from an elite shoemaker into a global fashion footwear producer with a worldwide network of boutiques.

FIGUEROA, BERNARD

Figueroa was born in France in 1961, and studied at the Studio Berçot in Paris. For his degree show he created a shoe decorated with abstract musical notes, fish and foliage, with a sculpted metal heel. This brought him to the attention of fashion designer Thierry Mugler, who commissioned Figueroa to design shoes for his collections. Figueroa subsequently designed footwear for Vera Wang, Coach, **CHARLES JOURDAN**, Adrienne Vittadini, **ROCKPORT** and Christian Dior, among others. In 1992 he launched his own bespoke couture line of shoes called Figueroa, known for their hand-sculpted heels. In 2000 Figueroa was appointed head of footwear design at Michael Kors, and in 2007 he became Payless ShoeSource's director of design for women's footwear.

FINSK

Finnish-born English designer Julia Lundsten launched her label Finsk in 2004, the year after graduating from London's Royal College of Art. Her father was an architect and her mother an interior designer, and they exposed Julia to modern design while growing up, an experience that is translated into her contemporary-looking shoes. Her environment-friendly designs use materials that are exotic but also sustainable.

FINSK
Platform ankle boots in black pony hair and multi-coloured suede with back zips and wedge heels, Autumn/Winter 2009

FLORSHEIM

Florsheim was founded as a retailer in Chicago in 1856 by the German émigré Sigmund Florsheim. Under his son the company moved into manufacturing men's quality footwear in 1892. The company ceased to be family owned when it was sold to Interco in 1953, by which time Florsheim was also making women's walking pumps and oxfords. In 1963 Florsheim controlled the majority of the American high-priced shoe market, but cheaper imports soon hit sales until the company was on the edge of bankruptcy in 1991. Florsheim entered the 'brown shoe' sport casuals market in 1993, but found only limited success. In 1999 all US production ceased and in 2002 the company was taken over by Weyco Group, a retail and wholesale distributor of men's brands, including Nunn Bush, Stacy Adams and Brass Boot.

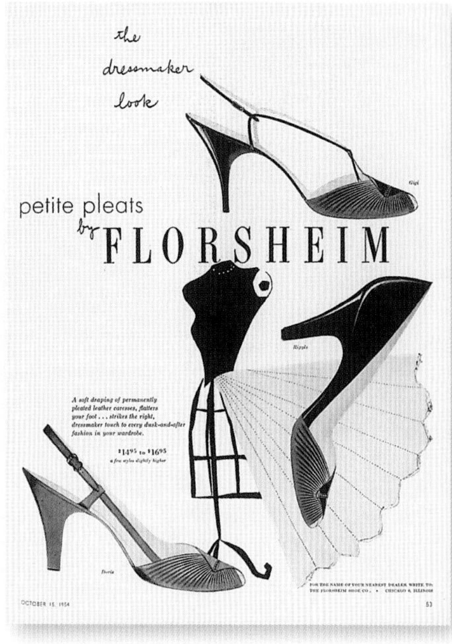

FLORSHEIM
Advertisement for Florsheim, Autumn 1954

FOX & FLUEVOG *see* **PETER FOX, JOHN FLUEVOG**

FRANÇOIS VILLON

François Villon (1911–97) was the professional name of the shoemaker Benveniste, who worked as a chief designer for **ANDRÉ PERUGIA**. In 1960 he opened his own design house at 27 rue du Faubourg Saint-Honoré, Paris. He produced thigh-high boots in the late 1960s, and during his career designed for couturiers including Louis Feraud, Hermès, Chanel, Lapidus, Patou, Ricci, Scherrer and Lanvin. Villon opened boutiques in Milan, New York, Singapore and Hong Kong and continued to work until his death.

FRANSI

Danish shoe manufacturer founded in 1936. Construction eventually moved to Italy and Spain while marketing and design remained headquartered in Copenhagen. The Billi Bi brand was launched by Fransi in 1993 for the Scandinavian market.

FRATELLI ROSSETTI

Renzo and Renato Rossetti set up Fratelli Rossetti in 1953 in Parabiago, near Milan. They became leaders in promoting Italian-made men's shoes for export in the 1960s (Italian women's shoes had been successfully exported since the 1950s). Success really came to the brothers when they translated the classic craftsmanship of men's footwear into a range of masculine-looking women's shoes in the 1970s. At the same time they launched a canvas-lined loafer that could be worn without socks. Renzo's three sons have expanded the brand and made it an international presence, with clients including Tom Cruise, Paloma Picasso and Lauren Bacall.

FRATELLI ROSSETTI
Advertisement for Fratelli Rossetti, Spring 1983

FRED SLATTEN

At the age of forty-eight, and after a career as a buyer for Nordstrom's department store, Fred Slatten opened his own shoe store in 1970 at 8803 Santa Monica Boulevard in West Hollywood. He designed unique lines for his boutique and offered the edgiest styles with the tallest platforms to the starlets, rock groups, centrefold models, and film and television studios of the Los Angeles area. Everyone from Sally Struthers to Elton John wore Fred Slatten shoes. The shop closed in 1992 but Fred Slatten continued freelance designing for the brands X-It and Pure Chocolat.

FRENCH SOLE
A selection of ballerina flats in metallic colours, 2010

FRYE
Contemporary leather boots based on nineteenth-century styles by Frye, including Campus (right), Harness (far right), and Jane Stitch (below), 2000s

FRENCH SOLE

Founded in 1989 by shoe designer Jane Winkworth, French Sole makes and sells ballerina flats. The business was originally run from Winkworth's basement in Chelsea, London. With Diana, the Princess of Wales, as one of Winkworth's most devoted fans, the business grew quickly, and a store opened in Fulham in 1991 and another in Sloane Street in 1997. French Sole shoes were originally made in France but some production has now gone to Spain. The company continues to produce only ballerina shoes, but in every imaginable material, colour and pattern.

FRYE

Founded in 1863, Frye is the oldest continuously operated shoe company in the United States, remaining under family ownership until 1945. The Frye Wellington boot worn by cavalry soldiers on both sides of the Civil War was one of the styles that led to the cowboy boot of the late nineteenth century. The original design, called the Campus, became popular again when it was reintroduced in the 1960s.

GABOR

Gabor is a family-owned company, founded in Barmstedt, near Hamburg, in 1949, and now headquartered in Rosenheim. Their fashion comfort boots and shoes are produced in Germany, Austria and, since the 1990s, in Portugal and the Slovak Republic.

GABRIELE SHOE FACTORY

Italian manufacturer originally established by Giovanni Beni in the 1930s and operated since 1988 by his grandson Gabriele Beni. In 1995 the company became known by its present name. It specializes in low-heeled fashionable walking footwear.

GAMBA

English theatrical dance footwear manufacturer Gamba has been located in Covent Garden, London, since 1903. Like most theatrical shoe suppliers, Gamba has discovered that it is a short leap from ballroom dance shoes to street shoes. Its fashion shoes have been on the market since at least the 1970s.

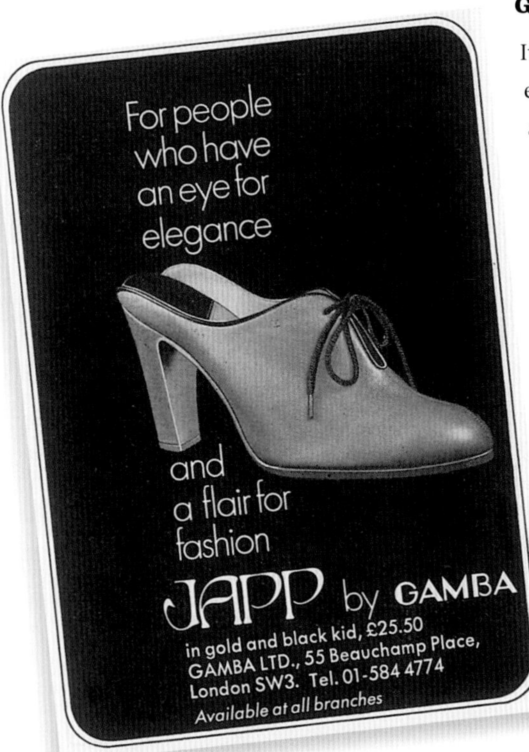

For people
who have
an eye for
elegance
and
a flair for
fashion
JAPP by GAMBA
in gold and black kid, £25.50
GAMBA LTD., 55 Beauchamp Place,
London SW3. Tel. 01-584 4774
Available at all branches

Put a fashionable
Spring in your step
with
GAMBA
Eros
Volta
Vivaldi
Ballin
Honeymoon
Heather
See the Spring and Summer 1976 range
of shoes at our own retail shops:
Gamba Ltd
46 Dean Street
London W1V 6HJ
Tel: (01) 437 0704
Gamba Ltd
55 Beauchamp Pl.
London SW3 1NY
Tel: (01) 584 4774
Gamba Ltd
4 Broomfield Hall
Chobham Road
Sunningdale
Berks
Tel: 0990 22796

GARDENIA

Founded in Copenhagen, Denmark, in 1941 with a line of wooden shoes, Gardenia grew during the 1950s to become a lucrative business. Shoes are produced under the labels Gardenia and the more fashion-forward line Shoebizz.

GAMBA

Above **Advertisement for Gamba, Spring 1976**

Left **Advertisement for Gamba, Autumn 1976**

GAROLINI

Albert and Bidi Finkelstein founded Garolini in 1970, though when Florence **OTWAY** began designing its line in 1974 she described it as a 'small company that produced ugly shoes'. After she left in 1976, Garolini's Italian-made shoes became a hit of the disco era and Garolini soon had the licences for making Halston and Fendi shoes. Andy Warhol was commissioned to create a stardust glitter-strewn photoprint of Garolini shoes for a *Vogue* advertisement. Garolini was bought by **UNITED STATES SHOE CORPORATION** in 1984.

GEMINI

Manufacturer founded by Bruno Meliani in 1971 near Pisa, Italy, producing women's fashion footwear for export to the US. The company today mainly produces two lines, Glitterpink and Gianna Meliani. The latter is named after its designer, the daughter of the founder, whose shoes often have vintage styling. The company retains a working relationship with many other famous labels such as Anne Klein, Anne Klein II, Yves Saint Laurent, **GUCCI**, Max Mara, Michael Kors, Burberry, Paul Smith and others. In 1998 Gianna Meliani opened her first store in Venice.

GEMINI GROUP

Founded by Vittorio Taffoni in 1969, the company was originally called La Torre (Italian for 'The Tower'), after a seventeenth-century tower adjacent to the company's building in the Marche region of Italy. The manufacturer was renamed Gemini Group and produces two fashion brands, La Torre and Cammina.

GAROLINI
Advertisement for Garolini, Spring 1983

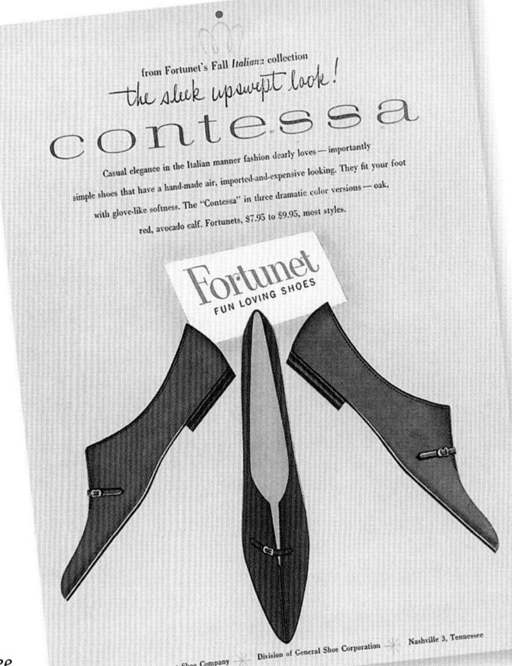

GENESCO
Advertisement for Contessa, one of the many brands of shoes produced by Genesco, Autumn 1955

GEORGE E. KEITH
Advertisement for Walk-Over, George E. Keith's leading brand for decades, Autumn 1950

GENESCO

The General Shoe Company was founded by James Jarman in 1924, and expanded under his son Maxey. As it prospered it bought other companies, such as Johnston & Murphy, Delman (*see* **HERMAN DELMAN**) and an American interest in **CHARLES JOURDAN**, as well as developing its own brands, such as Mademoiselle. The company became Genesco as it diversified into clothing, but by the 1990s it had refocused its efforts on men's footwear, such as western boots and the brand Nautica. Recent years have seen continued retrenchment in its operations. Today, Genesco operates the chain stores Dockers, Journeys and Underground Station, as well as Johnston & Murphy.

GEORGE E. KEITH

George E. Keith founded the company Green and Keith in Bridgewater, Massachusetts, in 1874. By the turn of the century its worldwide operation was exporting a line of men's Goodyear-welted shoes under the label Walk-Over, which from 1912 included women's designs. Under the Colby label the company became famous in the 1950s for its white bucks. Dexter shoes purchased the company in 1997.

GEORGINA GOODMAN
Stiletto-heel sandal with platform sole, Autumn/Winter 2009

GEORGINA GOODMAN

Born in 1965, Goodman worked as a stylist before studying shoe design at the London Cordwainers College from 1996. Her first line of shoes in 2003 featured uppers that looked as though they were made from orange peel, folded, moulded and stitched into shoes and boots. Her more recent collections offer both classic basics and contemporary couture styles.

GERARDINA DI MAGGIO

This Italian luxury brand was established in 1997 and is aimed at women who want sexy, high-quality, high-fashion footwear with an edge, as witnessed by their Rocker Chic 2010 collection.

GINA

Above and opposite **Rhinestone-encrusted platform pumps in peep-toe and closed-toe styles, Autumn/Winter 2009**

GIANMARCO LORENZI

This Italian company, with its showroom in Milan, began in the mid-1970s but came to prominence only in the late 1990s. It entered the US market in 2001, and is now sold worldwide through high-end venues. The collection is under the creative direction of Giovanni Renzi.

GIANNA MELIANI *see* GEMINI

GINA

Mehmet Kurdash's family had worked in the shoe industry since 1893. When he launched his footwear company in London in 1954, he named it after his favourite actress, Gina Lollobrigida. Today his sons Attila, Aydin and Altan design, manage and operate Gina and its two London shops on Sloane Street (since 1991) and Old Bond Street (since 1999).

GIORGIO MORETTO

Trademark brand name registered by Prada in 1986 for a line of women's shoes and bags.

GISAB

Manufacturer producing casual shoes with injection-moulded soles since 1965 in Barletta, Italy, under the brand names Eros, Comfort, Urt, New Sany, Free to Move and Trendy.

GIUSEPPE ZANOTTI

Born in San Mauro Pascoli, Italy, Zanotti worked as a design apprentice for Christian Dior and has been a consultant for Roberto Cavalli, Missoni and Vera Wang. In 1993 he launched his own eponymous label, followed by Vicini.

GIORGIO MORETTO
Advertisement for Giorgio Moretto, Spring 1986

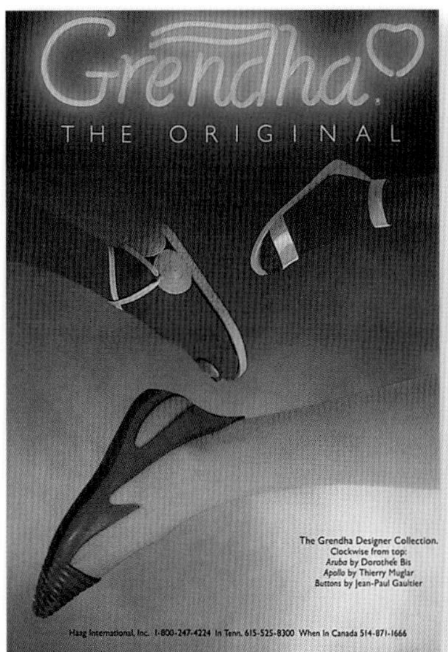

GOLO

German émigré Adolf Heilbrun founded the Golo Slipper Co. in New York in 1915. In the 1940s it developed women's casual Goodyear-welt shoes, but it took off as a force on the fashion-footwear scene in the 1960s, under the direction of the founder's grandson, Arthur Samuels Jr. He had trained under **DAVID EVINS** and he propelled Golo to become a leader in boots, especially gogo boots, famous for their style and innovative use of zippers and stretch fabrics. The company stopped making footwear in 1986 and the brand was later retired.

GRAVATI

Founded in 1909 in Milan to create high-quality men's dress shoes, Gravati now also makes women's laced shoes.

GRENDENE

Company founded in Farroupilha, Brazil, in 1971 by Alexandre and Pedro Grendene Bartelle to make plastic wine-bottle covers. It ventured into moulded plastic sandals called Jellies, which were a huge hit in the mid-1980s. The Melissa brand, founded in 1979, has been working in recent years with designers Judy Blame, Edson Matsuo, Alexandre Herchcovitch, and Fernando and Humberto Campana to create innovative plastic shoes for the international fashion market.

GRENDENE

Above **Advertisement for moulded jellies, Spring 1985**

Right **Moulded red plastic jellies made by Grendene under the Thierry Mugler label, 1985**

GREY MER
Patent pump with facetted heel,
Autumn/Winter 2009

GREY MER

Established in 1980 in San Mauro Pascoli, in the province of Forli-Cesena, Italy, Grey Mer manufactures up-market women's high-fashion footwear through its own label as well as Maggie Gi, a more youthful, affordable line.

GUCCI

The company's founder, Guccio Gucci (1881–1953), made saddles and luggage in Florence before the Second World War, experimenting with painted canvas when leather was scarce. On his death the family expanded the business, opening a store in New York in 1953 and in 1957 introducing a moccasin-constructed shoe with a gilded snaffle (instep chain strap, inspired by the founder's love of English equestrianism). The style was originally available just for men, in black or brown leather. In 1989 Gucci introduced an identical, but scaled-down, version for women in a variety of colours.

GUIDO PASQUALI

In 1967, after studying mechanics and engineering at Bocconi University in Milan, Guido Pasquali took over the business founded by his grandfather in 1918. During the 1970s he supplied shoes to Italian designers such as Walter Albini, Giorgio Armani and Missoni. His own trend-quality fashion footwear designs are available through his shop in Milan.

GUCCI
Advertisement for Gucci, Autumn 1979

GUIDO PASQUALI
Advertisement for Guido Pasquali, Autumn 1988

GUILLAUME HINFRAY

French-born designer Guillaume Hinfray gleans inspiration for his shoe designs from the past, referencing Vikings, Joan of Arc and German-occupied Paris. His work has been featured in haute couture collections from Hermès to Lanvin, and his shoes feature the highest quality in materials and craftmanship. In 1991 he was appointed head designer for women's shoes at **SALVATORE FERRAGAMO**, along with Marco Censi. Hinfray's shoes have appeared under the label Amaterasu since 2000 and under Guillaume Hinfray since 2003, as well as under other designer's labels, including Bottega Veneta and L'Autre Chose.

GUILLAUME HINFRAY
'Havre' platform sandal in suede and textile, Spring/Summer 2010

GUY RAUTUREAU *see* **RAUTUREAU**

GUILLAUME HINFRAY

Right 'Ylaire' black leather high heels with buckles and metallic details, Spring/Summer 2010

Below 'Vortex' black leather stiletto-heeled sandals with ankle straps, Spring/Summer 2010

H. & R. RAYNE

From beginnings as a theatrical supplier in the 1880s Rayne grew to be a shoe manufacturer with a royal warrant in the 1930s. The company had been among the first to involve itself in licensing agreements and in 1957 arranged to produce **ROGER VIVIER'S** designs for Christian Dior. Through similar arrangements with Wedgwood in 1959 and 1978 Rayne made shoes with heels featuring the pottery manufacturer's famous jasperware design. Under head designer Jean Matthew, Rayne created shoe collections for apparel designers including Hardy Amies, Norman Hartnell, Mary Quant, Bill Gibb, Bruce Oldfield and Jean Muir. The company was sold in 1973 to Debenhams department stores but poor business decisions led to drift and Rayne lost ground to its competitors, becoming a retailer rather than a supplier. It eventually closed in 1994.

H. H. BROWN

Founded in 1883 in Massachusetts by Henry H. Brown, the company was sold in 1927 to Ray Heffernan, who ran it until 1989. In 1991 Warren Buffet bought the company and H. H. Brown became a subsidiary of Berkshire Hathaway. In 2002 a women's comfort line was spun off into a division under the company name of Sofft. Today H. H. Brown's casual, work and dress shoes and boots are sold under the brand names Acme, Brunswick, Carolina, Corcoran, Dexter, Double-H, Matterhorn, Quark and Ruhne. The company also produces shoes under the Bøc and **BØRN** labels.

HELLSTERN

Founded by Louis Hellstern in Paris in the 1870s, the company became known for its quality men's and women's footwear. Under Louis' son Charles the company was at its height of success in the 1920s, producing elegant day and evening footwear, and with boutiques in Brussels, London and Cannes. The company went into decline following the Second World War, and its last boutique closed in 1970. The shoes were exclusive and the few pairs that still exist have been donated to museums, with their matching couture gowns.

H. & R. RAYNE
Above **Advertisement for H. & R. Rayne, Summer 1974**

Opposite **Rhinestone-decorated white silk evening shoes by 'Miss Rayne', part of H. & R. Rayne, early 1960s**

Miss Rayne

HERBERT LEVINE

In 1948 journalist Herbert Levine (1916–91) and his wife, shoe model Beth (1914–2006), started their own shoe company. Herbert was the business manager while Beth designed the shoes. In 1954, with only six years of collections behind them, the Levines received a Neiman Marcus Award for their contribution to shoe design. The Herbert Levine Company introduced the world to Spring-o-Lator mules and stocking boots (tights or pantyhose with attached soles and heels) in the 1950s. They also popularized the return of the fashion boot in the 1960s, for which the company received a Coty award in 1967. The Levines' strength lay in anticipating trends, like the pointed toe of 1957. Fun heels, rhinestone-covered pumps and the use of new, space-age materials like vinyl and acrylic were trademarks of the Herbert Levine look. In 1964 Beth designed the aerodynamic 'Kabuki' pumps, which gave the illusion that the wearer was walking on air. Levine designed shoes for three American first ladies, Jacqueline Kennedy, Lady Bird Johnson and Patricia Nixon, as well as the famous white go-go boots Nancy Sinatra wore while singing 'These boots are made for walkin' in 1966. Although the Levines received another Coty award in 1973, a changing marketplace and foreign imports were the catalyst for the company's closure in 1975.

HERBERT LEVINE
Above left **Red suede and gilded wood platform 'Kabuki' pumps, 1964**

Above **Advertisement for Herbert Levine, Summer 1954**

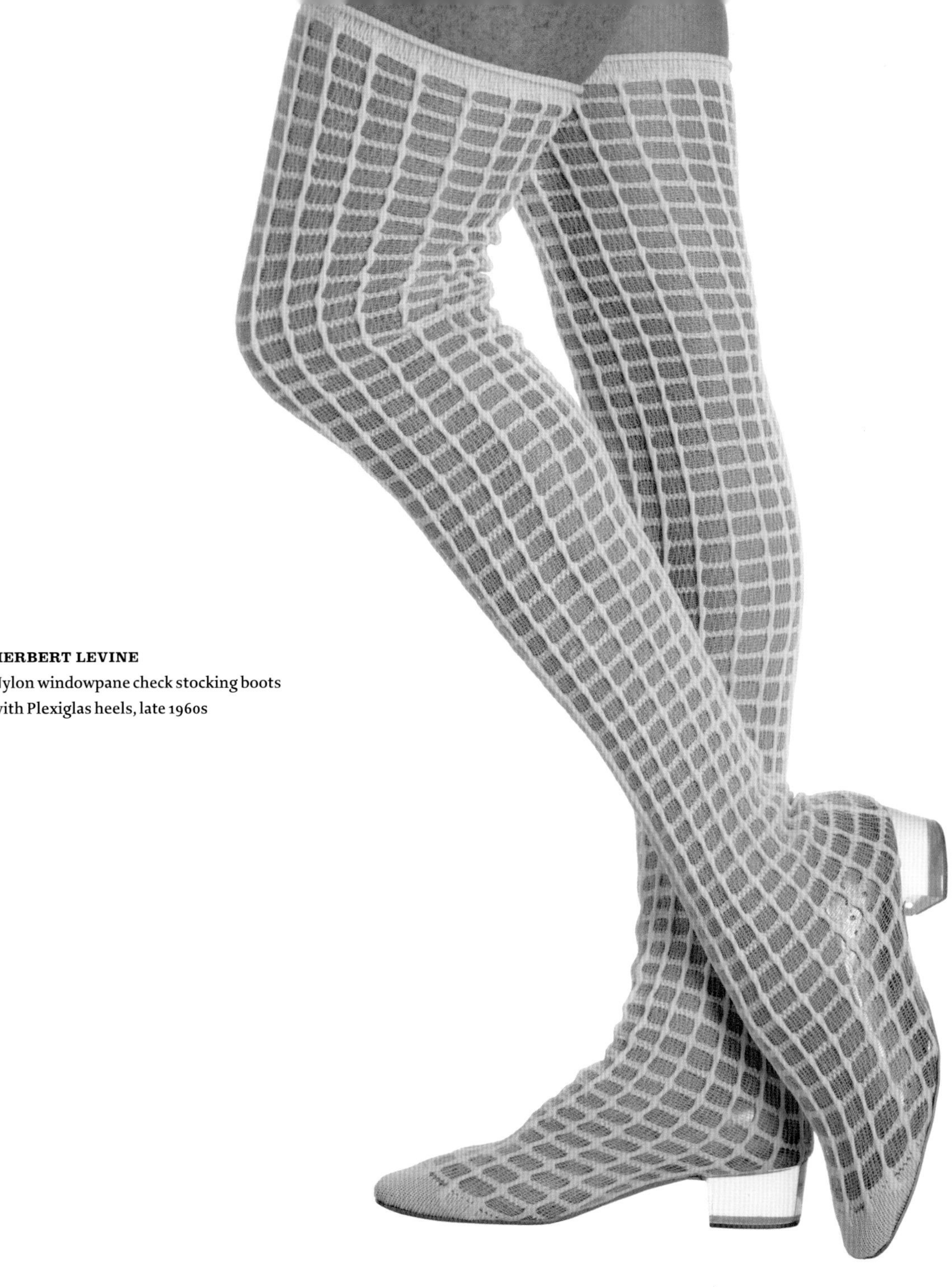

HERBERT LEVINE
Nylon windowpane check stocking boots with Plexiglas heels, late 1960s

BEAUTIFUL SHOEMANSHIP FOR FALL-WINTER DESIGNED BY THE MASTER
DELMAN
Bergdorf Goodman New York and other fine stores across the nation

HERMAN DELMAN

Left Advertisement for Herman Delman, Autumn 1952

Below Pink lace and leather pumps, *c.* 1960

HERMAN DELMAN
Red rhinestone pavé pumps, mid-1960s

HERMAN DELMAN

Born in 1895, Herman Delman was the son of a shoe-store owner in Portland, Oregon. Delman began his business with a shoe store on Madison Avenue in New York in 1919. His success was due to his rare combined ability to recognize design talent while also having great business acumen. He understood the necessity of printing his name in his shoes so that wherever they were sold, including at top retailers like Bergdorf Goodman, his name would become a recognized brand. In 1936 he formed a licensing agreement with **H. & R. PAYNE** to produce Delman shoes for the English market, and in 1938 he spied the young talent of **ROGER VIVIER** and bought many of his designs for the Delman label. In 1954 he sold his business to Genesco. The brand continued to prosper into the 1960s, but began to lose ground in the 1970s, finally closing in 1988. In 1989 **NINA FOOTWEAR INC.** acquired the Delman name with plans to revive its tradition of elegant quality footwear.

HESTER VAN EEGHEN
Blue leather cutaway 'Ludwig' design with lacing by Leo Potma for Hester van Eeghen, 2009

HEYRAUD
Advertisement for Heyraud, Autumn 1974

HESTER VAN EEGHEN

Amsterdam-based Hester van Eeghen has been designing leather accessories for sale in shops across Europe since 1988 but only in 2000 began designing high-fashion forward line shoes, which are handmade in Italy.

HEYRAUD

Heyraud was founded in France in 1927 as a modern shoe manufacturer to produce fashion footwear using American machines and mass-production techniques. From the 1930s to the 1950s its Preciosa brand competed with **BALLY** and similar high-end ready-made footwear. In 1993 the company became a division of ERAM, a French clothing company.

HILL AND DALE *see* DUNN & MCCARTHY

HÖGL *see* LORENZ SHOE GROUP

HOLMES OF NORWICH

Henry Nicholas Holmes was born in Norwich, England, in 1868. After apprenticing in the boot and shoe industry he formed a partnership in 1891 with W. E. Edwards, operating out of the Edwards' home. The business grew to become one of the largest shoe manufacturers in England, producing shoes under the label Edward and Holmes as well as Holmes of Norwich. It later became part of the British Shoe Corporation.

HUSH PUPPIES *see* WOLVERINE

HOLMES OF NORWICH
Black suede pumps with silver filigree wedge heels, *c.* 1958

I. MILLER

Israel Miller was born in Russia and moved to the United States, where he was taught by an Italian shoemaker in New York. In 1880 he established what would become a family company, opening a store and factory on 23rd Street, making and selling theatrical footwear. By the 1940s the company had become known for its fashion footwear, created by freelance designers such as **ANDRÉ PERUGIA** and **DAVID EVINS**, as well as its own growing studio of talent, including Margaret Clark (*see* **MARGARET JERROLD**). The company is often remembered for hiring the young Andy Warhol in the late 1950s to dress windows and produce charming shoe sketches used for Christmas greeting cards. By the 1960s I. Miller had entered the youth market with a line called Miller Eye. In 1973 the company was sold to **GENESCO**,where it became part of the Rayne division until the early 1980s when it was liquidated.

ICON

In November 1999 Neiman Marcus offered shoes printed with Andy Warhol's Campbell's Soup labels for $260 per pair. The creator of the shoes, Peter Traynor, had developed a process for printing artwork onto casual leather and the shoes became an immediate hit when they were worn by Hollywood stars. By 2001 the shoes were being retailed across the US and internationally under the Icon label.

A bright new I. Miller idea
in Fleming-Joffe leather,
individually hand-ombréd to
blend with your
dominant new costume color.
A DIVISION OF GENERAL SHOE CORP.
MUTATION BY I. Miller

I. MILLER
Advertisement for I. Miller, Spring 1958

INTERNATIONAL SHOE COMPANY
Advertisement for Accent Shoes, a brand made by International Shoe Company, Summer 1959

ILIAN FOSSA

In 1972 Pazzi Alberto started a shoe company in Porto Sant'Elpidio, Italy, and in 1988 created the brand Ilian Fossa, which is now operated by his sons Simone and Andrea.

INTERNATIONAL SHOE COMPANY

The St. Louis based International Shoe Company was created by the amalgamation of smaller companies in 1911, and continued to grow through acquisition over the years. Its most popular women's shoe brands in the 1950s and 1960s were **QUEEN QUALITY AND VITALITY**. In 1953 International Shoe acquired ownership of the **FLORSHEIM SHOE COMPANY**, and in 1954 it acquired all the common stock of Savage Shoes of Canada. By 1961 the company had ninety-one footwear-manufacturing facilities, tanneries and warehouses, employing over 33,000 people. The company diversified into furniture manufacturing, renaming itself Interco in 1966. In 1984 the decline in domestic footwear production combined with a recession caused Interco to begin reorganizing its holdings. Converse was acquired in 1986, but the footwear division – except for Florsheim – was otherwise dissolved in 1987. All footwear production ceased in 1994 when Florsheim and Converse were sold.

IRREGULAR CHOICE

In the seaside town of Brighton on the south coast of England, designer Dan Sullivan launched his shoe store Irregular Choice in 1999. There are now shops in London and New York, catering to the Japanese-Gothic-Lolita aesthetic of fun, colourful footwear. Sullivan designs exclusive lines for his label, sometimes in limited editions with numbered pairs. A men's line was added in 2004.

IRREGULAR CHOICE
Above left **Black and white chevron-printed ankle boot, 2009**

Above **Floral-trimmed 'Courtesan pink' pump, 2009**

ISABELLA ZOCCHI
Sketches for shoe designs, 2009

ISABELLA ZOCCHI

Born in Varese, Italy, in 1976, Zocchi apprenticed at her family's gold jewelry company and worked as a jewelry designer before going to the European Institute of Design in Milan to complete a course in shoe design. Her shoe collections are influenced by sculptural practices, and are individually handcrafted in Italy.

J. RENEÉ

Founded in the late 1970s, J. Reneé and Jessica Bennett shoes are designed in Carrollton, Texas. The J. Reneé brand aims to be affordable, stylish and comfortable; Jessica Bennett is aimed at a fashion-forward audience.

JACK ROGERS

In the early 1960s Harry Rabin, a businessman from Palm Beach, Florida, formed a company with Jack Rogers, a former sales agent for Saks Fifth Avenue. They hired a local Florida cobbler to create sandals based on a Navajo Indian design, which they sold wholesale under the brand name Jack Rogers Navajos. The shoes were distributed through the Saks Fifth Avenue stores and became a fashion sensation after Jacqueline Kennedy was photographed wearing a pair in 1962. They became her vacation staple, and have remained a fashion mainstay.

JACQUES KEKLIKIAN

Born in Turkey in 1911, Keklikian worked for his brother, a cobbler, in the 1920s. He moved to St Tropez, France, in 1933 and began to make simple sandals from greased (waterproof) leather, inspired by designs from ancient statues. He signed his products 'K. Jacques' and built a reputation making his sandals for holidaying tourists, including Colette, Brigitte Bardot, Jean Cocteau and Pablo Picasso. His sandals have been used on the catwalk by clothes designers Jean Charles de Castelbajac, Kenzo and Helmut Lang.

JACK ROGERS
'Navajo' leather thong sandals in different colours, 2000s

JACQUES LEVINE
Embroidered linen sling-back pumps, late 1960s

JACQUES LEVINE

Company founded in 1936 by Falk Levine in Middletown, New York, as Middletown Footwear. It soon made a hit with marabou-trimmed boudoir slippers, a style still in production. The founder's son, Jacques Levine, created a successful line of fashion footwear in the 1950s that bore his name, but in the 1970s the brand became dowdy. Jacques' son Harold now manages the company and is revitalizing the brand.

JAN JANSEN

Below and opposite **Stiletto-heeled and platform-soled glossy red shoes and boots, 2009**

JAN JANSEN

Born in Holland in 1941, Jansen began his design career in 1964, working for **JEANNOT**. In 1969 he created the Woody, a clog sole with leather upper. It was so widely copied that Jansen abandoned the design, but it had set a fashion for the return of clogs in the 1970s. His high-heeled sneaker was the next big hit in the late 1970s, selling a million pairs in the US alone. By the 1980s Jansen was designing six collections a year, some brand named, which were sold around the world. One of the most successful was the Bruno line. In the 1990s he started to produce shoes under his own name that explored his avant-garde side, with designs that combined architectural and sculptural elements. In 1996 he received the title of Grand Seigneur, the top Dutch fashion prize, for his contribution to the national and international fashion scene.

JEAN-BAPTISTE RAUTUREAU *see* RAUTUREAU

JEANNOT

Company founded in 1946 in Molfetta, Italy, by Giovanni Porta. Jeannot produces women's medium- to high-price fashion footwear.

JENNE O
Laced leather thigh-high boots, hand-painted by illustrator Sarah Howell, part of a series of boots designed by Jenne O and painted by artists, late 2000s

JENNE O

American-born Jennefer Osterhoudt studied at Parsons School of Design in New York and Paris. She worked with John Galliano in Paris, eventually as his chief accessories designer. Osterhoudt then designed shoes for Alexander McQueen at Givenchy, before moving to London to be McQueen's head of accessories. In 2003 she launched her own line of burlesque-inspired shoes under the label Jenne O.

JERRY EDOUARD

Although its footwear was labelled 'made in Greece', the provenance of Jerry Edouard is obscure. Its boots and shoes were of excellent quality and were sold through high-end shops and clothing stores in the US between 1968 and 1972.

JERRY EDOUARD
Cream leather and snakeskin pumps, *c.* 1969

JIMMY CHOO

Left Flat black sandals with stud and eyelet motif by Jimmy Choo for H&M, 2009

Below Metallic blue stiletto high heel with back zip by Jimmy Choo for H&M, 2009

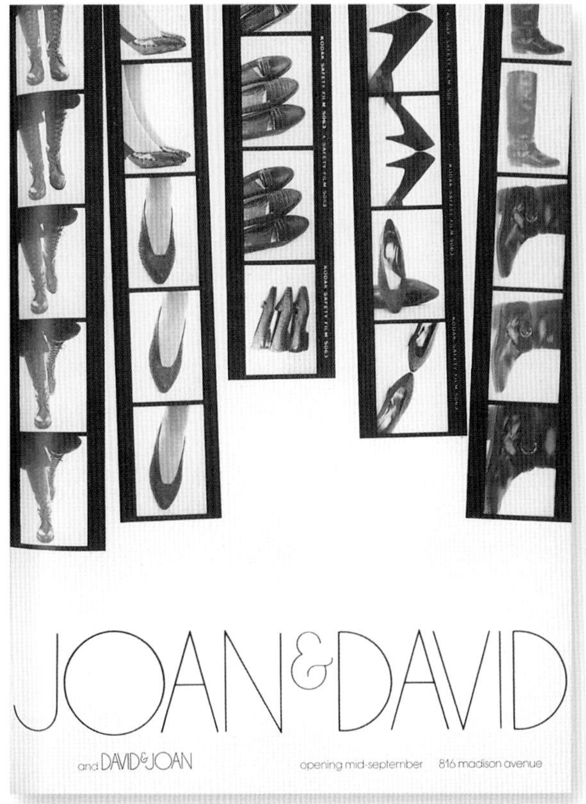

JOAN & DAVID
Advertisement for Joan & David, Autumn 1985

JIMMY CHOO

Choo was born into a family of Malaysian shoemakers in 1961 and made his first pair of shoes when he was eleven years old. He graduated from Cordwainers College and the London College of Fashion in 1989, and began to make bespoke footwear in the early 1990s. His most famous client was Princess Diana, for whom he made 'countless' pairs; she was frequently seen wearing his high-heeled shoes after her separation from Prince Charles. In 1996 Choo launched a line of Italian-made ready-to-wear shoes, in partnership with Tamara Yeardye, former British *Vogue* accessories editor. In 1998 they opened their first boutique in New York. Irreconcilable differences developed between the two that were not kept discrete, and Choo eventually sold out his share in 2001, just before the company expanded into handbags; he has not been connected to the creative side of the Jimmy Choo label since. In 2003 Choo was awarded an OBE for his contribution to making London a fashion design centre. Through astute business direction, the Jimmy Choo company has continued to gain momentum and brand recognition, and as of 2010 there are 100 Jimmy Choo stores worldwide.

JOAN & DAVID

David Halpern was chairman of Suburban Shoe Stores when he met and married Joan, a Harvard psychology student. She began at a small Boston company, designing neutral-toned pumps and oxfords with sensible heels for the modern liberated woman. The label Joan & David was launched in 1977 and the following year Joan was awarded a Fashion Critics' Coty award for design. A men's line, David and Joan, was launched in 1982, and a less expensive line, Joan & David Too, in 1987. They opened a shoe store on Madison Avenue, New York, in 1985, and from there an empire of stores, franchises and boutiques in department stores has grown. The company is now based in Italy.

JOHANSEN

Company founded in 1876 in St. Louis, Missouri. The Johansen brothers made women's dress and casual shoes until the factory closed in June 1999.

JOHN FLUEVOG

Twenty-two-year-old John Fluevog opened an avant-garde shoe store in Vancouver in 1970 with English shoemaker and designer Peter Fox. Their boots and shoes were aimed at a stylish youthful market, appealing to followers of glam-rock. The two went their separate creative ways in 1980 and Fluevog opened an eponymous store in Seattle in 1986, followed quickly by others in Toronto and Boston. His designs are manufactured by George Cox in England and are aimed at the street fashion crowd. Since the 1980s punks, goths and rockabillies have worn Fluevog shoes. He also designs for the European manufacturer Dynamic, which produces Fluevog brand shoes for the European, Japanese and Australian markets. Designers Comrags, Anna Sui and Betsey Johnson have used his shoes.

JOHANSEN

Opposite top Advertisement for Johansen shoes, Spring 1957

JOHN FLUEVOG

Opposite bottom A page from John Fluevog's Autumn 1998 catalogue

Right and below Leather shoes with the signature John Fluevog splayed heels, Autumn 1992

JOHNNY MOKE

John Joseph Rowley was born in London in 1945 and educated at McKentie Technical College. With his friend Mick Oram he opened a vintage clothing shop in 1967 in the basement of a King's Road boutique called Granny Takes a Trip. Rowley and Oram moved to Kensington Market at about the same time Johnny purchased a small car called a Mini Moke, from which he took his last name. The Kensington shop stocked merchandise from new designers, including snakeskin platform sandals from then unknown **TERRY DE HAVILLAND**. After a break from the fashion world in the 1970s Moke opened a shop called Ad Hoc, which sold his own clothes and shoes. In 1984 Johnny Moke opened his eponymous shop at 396 King's Road, where he made shoes for clients including Boy George, Tom Cruise, Tim Roth and Gary Oldman, and even a pair for Glenn Close for her 1996 film *101 Dalmatians*. He gained some notoriety in 1997 after he appeared on television denouncing the wearing of trainers: 'You don't wear a bikini in the supermarket, so why wear a sports shoe on the high street?' His outburst brought him public support and business. Moke's shop closed in 2002 and he died in 2009.

JOHNNY MOKE
Two shoe designs with sculptural elements, 1980s

JOHNSON, STEPHENS AND SHINKLE SHOE COMPANY
Advertisement for Lullabies brand by Johnson, Stephens and Shinkle Shoe Company, Spring 1950

JOHNSON, STEPHENS AND SHINKLE SHOE COMPANY

The Johnson, Stephens and Shinkle Shoe Company was founded in St. Louis, Missouri, by Bradford Shinkle, his brother-in-law Andrew Johnson and his friend Howard Stephens. The company was known for its brand Rhythm Step, until its demise in the early 1970s.

JONES APPAREL GROUP

Founded in 1970 and renamed in 1975 as Jones Apparel Group. The company went public in 1991 and acquired the Evan Picone label in 1993, Nine West in 1999, and Maxwell Shoe Co. in 2004. Today it is the parent company of numerous shoe brands and clothing lines with associated shoe brands including, **NINE WEST**, Easy Spirit, Bandolino, Enzo **ANGIOLINI**, **JOAN & DAVID**, Mootsies Tootsies, **SAM & LIBBY**, Anne Klein, Gloria Vanderbilt and LEI (Life, energy, intelligence).

JOSEF SEIBEL

Shoemaking company founded in 1886. It makes comfort and casual shoes under its own brand name as well as **ROMIKA**. Westland, which Seibel acquired in 1996, is a long-established manufacturer of men's dress shoes.

JOSEPH AZAGURY

Born in the early 1960s in Morocco, Azagury moved to London as a young man and trained at Cordwainers College. He learned the footwear trade while selling shoes in the Rayne department at Harrods. Azagury opened his first store in London in 1991, selling Italian-made shoes for women, with a focus upon high-end fashion and bridal designs.

JULIANELLI

In 1947 New Yorker husband-and-wife team Charles and Mabel Julianelli teamed up to create Julianelli shoes, with Charles in charge of production and Mabel heading design. In addition to her own line, Mabel also designed for other companies, including DeLiso Debs (*see* **PALTER DELISO**). She became known for light and airy sandals with a feminine touch, even in her low-heeled designs. Recognized in 1950 with a Coty award, Mabel continued to design for the high end of the American shoe industry until 1987.

JUSTIN BOOT COMPANY

Having begun as a boot repairer on the Chisholm Trail in Texas in 1879 H. J. Justin started making boots for cowboys in Nocona, Texas. His children continued the family tradition, which was still flourishing by the time of the Tex-Mex fashion revival of the early 1990s. Following a peak in 1993, sales began to fall, and the company moved its operations to El Paso, and to Cassville, Missouri. Justin had acquired the Nocona Boot Company, established by the founder's daughter, in 1981, as well as **TONY LAMA** in 1990. The family connection ended in 2000, shortly before the death of John Justin, the founder's grandson.

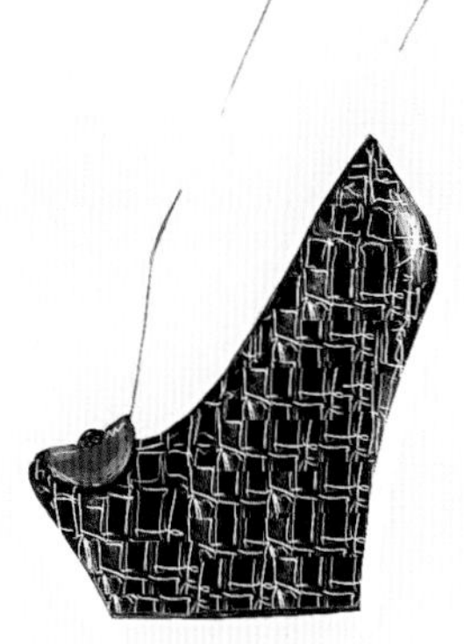

JOSEPH AZAGURY
Designs for shoes by Joseph Azagury, Summer 2007

JULIANELLI

Below Advertisement for Julianelli shoes, Spring 1985

Below right Brown satin and black velvet brocade pumps, late 1950s

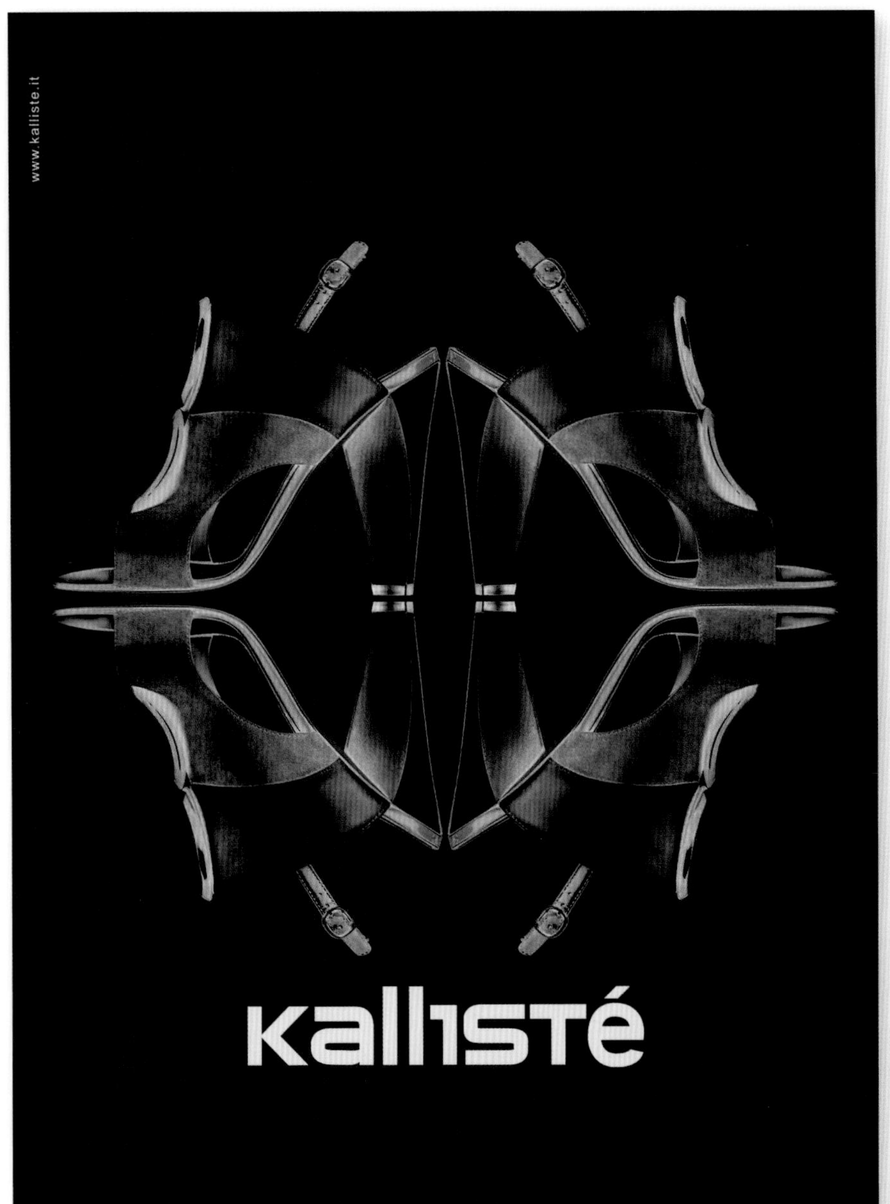

KALLISTÉ
Advertisement for Kallisté, Spring/
Summer 2009

KENNETH COLE
Advertisement for Kenneth Cole, Autumn 1994

KARINE ARABIAN
'Anahide' black boot in leather and velvet with laser-cut metallic-leather lining, late 2000s

KALLISTÉ

High-fashion footwear brand named after the founder of a workshop in 1952. In 2002 the brand Key-te was launched for the younger client. In 2005 the company was taken over by Calzaturificio Mima, which continues the Kallisté brand with a flagship store in Milan.

KALSO, ANNE *see* EARTH SHOES

Lace Up Ankle Boot
"We support artistic freedom and creative license but draw the line at nude footage."
—Kenneth Cole

KARINE ARABIAN

After gaining recognition at the Hyères Festival of Fashion Design and Photography in 1993, French designer Karine Arabian began designing shoes for Swarovski and Chanel. Arabian opened her Paris showroom and boutique in 2001, featuring her own brand of shoes, bags and jewelry.

KENNEL & SCHMENGER

Founded in 1918 in Pirmasens, Germany, Kennel & Schmenger today produces half a million pairs of casual and high-fashion shoes per year, primarily for the domestic and European market.

KENNETH COLE

Kenneth Cole has distinguished itself by acute branding of affordable up-to-date fashion footwear. Its founder made a name for himself while working for his father's leather products company, El Greco. **ARMANDO POLLINI** had designed a simple mule with leather straps and a solid bottom called **CANDIES**, and Kenneth Cole spotted its potential, importing more than 10 million pairs into the US in 1978 and 1979.

A NEW MOVEMENT AFOOT...Step into a jet and—*whoosh!*—you're in Paris. Easier still, just step into an Enzel of Paris shoe. This promenade pump, for example, shown in marron doré; also in Parisian black and olivâtre green. Just one of many styles in the new Enzel collection for Fall. 10.99 and 12.99.
Exclusively at Kinney's
Enzel
OF PARIS

Wanting to explore a higher-end market, Cole left his father's company to form his own supply and import business in 1982. For marketing reasons he called his company Kenneth Cole Productions, exploiting a by-law in New York City which allowed film production companies to park large trailers in midtown Manhattan during shoe-market week. The company's first brand was What's What, followed in 1987 by the junior line Unlisted. Cole opened his first eponymous store in New York in 1985, and in 1992 began supplying a private label for American retailers Sears and J C Penney. The Reaction line of shoes was launched in 1994, the same year the company went public and branched into clothing lines. Though now a multi-billion dollar company, Kenneth Cole has continued to distinguish itself through political, socially conscious and humorous marketing campaigns, using witty, and occasionally controversial, advertising to raise awareness of issues such as AIDS and homelessness.

KINNEY SHOES

Left Advertisement for Kinney Shoes, Autumn 1960

Below Advertisement for Kinney Shoes, Autumn 1974

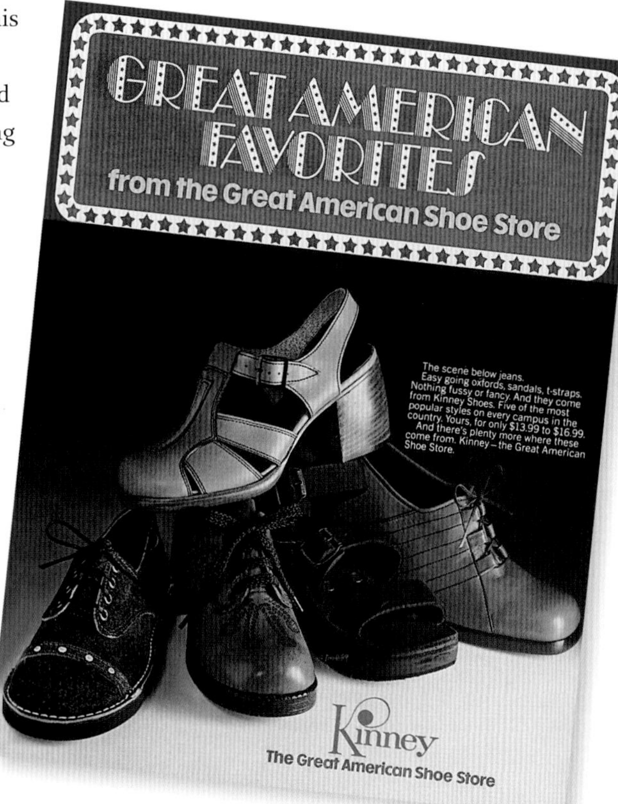

GREAT AMERICAN FAVORITES
from the Great American Shoe Store
The scene below jeans.
Easy going oxfords, sandals, t-straps. Nothing fussy or fancy. And they come from Kinney Shoes. Five of the most popular styles on every campus in the country. Yours, for only $13.99 to $16.99.
And there's plenty more where these come from. Kinney – the Great American Shoe Store.

The Great American Shoe Store

KICKERINOS

Founded in Milwaukee, Wisconsin, in 1946, the company was known for its brand of fleece-lined boots with crêpe rubber soles produced between 1953 and 1984.

KICKERS

English company founded in 1970 by Daniel Raufast to manufacture footwear for the blue-jean generation. Designer Jacques Chevallereau created the 'jean boot', a short boot made of nubuck, with crêpe soles and contrasted stitching comparable with blue-jean design. By 1974 Kickers were selling internationally. The company is now a division of Pentland Brand Plc.

KINNEY SHOES

Founded in 1894 by George Romanta Kinney, the company manufactured and retailed shoes for over a century, starting with one store in Waverly, New York, but quickly expanding. Kinney exploited economies of scale to beat its competitors' prices. The company was finally bought out by Brown Shoe Company, then by F. W. Woolworth in 1963. Divisions were added, including Stylco in 1967, Susie Casuals in 1968 and Footlocker in 1974. Family-oriented chain-store shoe shopping began falling from favour during the 1970s and eventually led to the closure of Kinney in 1998.

KICKERS
'Kick Hi' short boot in nubuck leather, 2009

KRON BY KRONKRON

Left Pink leather platform shoe with front zip, 2009

Below Multi-coloured laced platform shoe in leather and suede, 2009

KRISTEN LEE
Advertisement for Kristen Lee, *c.* 2009

KRISTEN LEE

Established in 2002, Kristen Lee works out of Los Angeles and Brooklyn reviving and updating women's vintage shoe styles for today's fashion shoe buyer.

KRON BY KRONKRON

Hugrún Árnadóttir and Magni Porsteinsson are Icelandic designers who opened the shoe store Kron in Reykjavik in 2000. In 2008 they launched their own contemporary line, which is made in Spain.

KUMAGAI *see* TOKIO KUMAGAI

LADY DOC

Brand made by Calzature Doc, a manufacturer founded in the late 1970s by Renzo Tosoni in Civitanova Marche, Italy, that produces fashion and casual footwear. There is a men's line called Mister Doc.

LA MARCA

Italian-born Erasmo La Marca and his American-born wife Arlene Zubritzky were a team who designed shoes under the brand name La Marca. The shoes were made in Italy and imported into the US for sale in high-end boutiques including their own store, La Marca Shoes, on 57th street in Manhattan from 1970 to 1990.

LARIO

In 1898 Gerolamo Saibene established a small workshop making simple footwear for local farmers in the town of Cirimido, near Como, Italy. The men's footwear company expanded and became incorporated in 1925. The majority of Lario's output went to the American market in the 1950s; in 1965 women's shoes were added to their line, but mostly for the European market. The company also produces shoes under licence for Giorgio Armani, Cerruti 1881, Trussardi, Jil Sander, Etro, Blumarine and others. Lario is still under family operation and now exports 70 per cent of the 90,000 pairs of shoes it produces each year.

LAURENCE DACADE

French shoe designer Laurence Dacade trained at the Afpic School of Shoe Design in Paris and soon after graduating won design jobs with major French fashion houses including Balmain, Lacroix, Lagerfeld and Givenchy. She started her own label in 2002 with the philosophy that women need not suffer to be beautiful. However, her fondness for sexy high-fashion results in styles that aren't exactly orthopaedic!

LA MARCA
Advertisement for La Marca shoes, Spring 1983

LAURENCE DACADE
'Omage' leather and lace sandal, 2009

LAZZERI

Located near Florence, Lazzeri was established in the late 1960s and named after the founder. Current lines produced at Lazzeri include Lazzeri Manifatture for classic styles, and Hal for casual shoes. Lazzeri also manufactures footwear for Banana Republic and John Varvatos.

LD TUTTLE

Tuttle graduated from the Fashion Institute of Technology in New York and Milan's Ars Arpel School. She established her label LD Tuttle in 2004, including her husband's initials, L. D., in the brand. Her shoes have been described as 'utilitarian glamour' with designs that are chic but not excessive in their style. She lives in Los Angeles but travels frequently to Italy where her shoes are manufactured.

LE SILLA

Italian designer Enio Silla established his company in 1994, producing high-heeled, high-fashion shoes.

LE SILLA
Rhinestone-encrusted sandals and studded leather boot, 2009

LERRE

Though the company was founded in 1939, few had heard of Lerre because it made shoes for other labels. In 1972 it manufactured Santini and **DOMINICI FOOTWEAR**, but when that design team broke up in 1985 an agreement was struck with Ernesto Esposito, who was already designing collections for Max Mara, Sergio Rossi and Benetton. Esposito's boots and shoes created under the Lerre brand were aimed at 30–50-year-old women but the up-market collection found only moderate success. Lerre went back to making collections under other labels, like Todd Oldham, alongside their own brand.

LERRE
Advertisement for Lerre, Autumn 1993

LIFESTRIDE *see* BROWN SHOE COMPANY

LILLEY & SKINNER

The English shoe retailer Lilley & Skinner began as the firm Thomas Lilley in 1835 in Southwark, London. In 1881 Lilley took his son-in-law William Banks Skinner into partnership and changed the firm's name. The company was taken over by the British Shoe Corporation in the 1950s, along with Manfield, Dolcis, Saxone and other shoe companies but the label survives as a store brand.

LINEA MARCHE

Established in 1972 in the Marche region of Italy, the company originally manufactured safety shoes. In 1980 it began manufacturing footwear for chain stores and large companies all over Europe. In 1987 the first in-house fashion

brand was launched, called Aketohn. Edgier brands followed, including Vic Matie (for women) and Paul May (for men), and in 1991 OXS was launched, aimed at the trendy youth market. In 1992 the production manager, Renato Curzi, bought the company and continues to operate it as managing director.

LOEFFLER RANDALL

Manufacturer launched in New York in 2005 by husband and wife Brian Murphy and Jessie Randall. The idea to start a shoe company had come from Jessie, who was frustrated by looking for trendy, well-made shoes that were also understated and elegant. The brand met with immediate commercial and critical success.

LOEFFLER RANDALL

Far left **'Yvette' cutout ankle boot in multi-coloured suede with concealed platform and back zip, late 2000s**

Left **'Matilde' flat pull-on boot in black leather with embossed anaconda texture and a tapered toe, late 2000s**

LORENZ SHOE GROUP

The parent company of the brands Högl, Ganter and Hassia is located in Taufkirchen and der Pram in Upper Austria and is one of the largest shoe manufacturers in Europe. Högl has been active in the international shoe market for over seventy years and currently exports about 90 per cent of its shoes to thirty countries around the world.

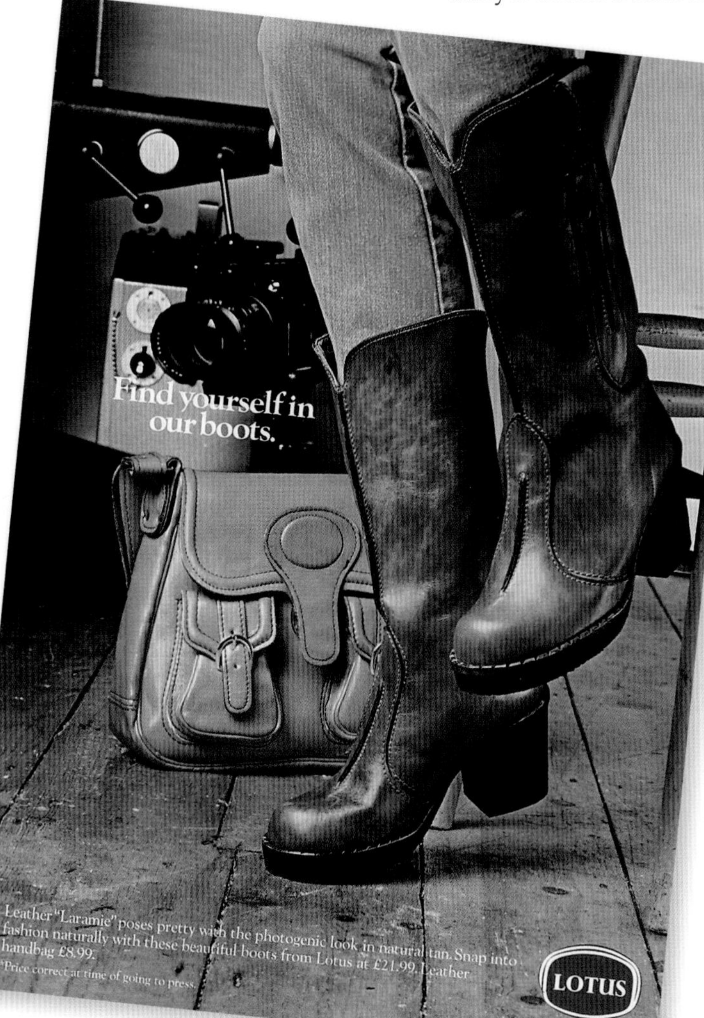

Find yourself in our boots.
Leather "Laramie" poses pretty with the photogenic look in natural tan. Snap into fashion naturally with these beautiful boots from Lotus at £21.99. Leather handbag £8.99.
*Price correct at time of going to press.
LOTUS

LOTUS
Advertisement for Lotus, Autumn 1976

LORENZO BANFI

Established in the 1970s in Parabiago, close to Milan, Lorenzo Banfi is a luxury brand manufacturer of hand-finished men's and women's shoes sold through elite retailers.

LOTUS

Stafford, like Northampton, was once a large shoemaking centre in England. Its largest manufacturer was Lotus, a company that emerged from the amalgamation of three smaller companies in 1919. By the 1970s Lotus was the last remaining shoe manufacturer in the town, but competition from imports took their toll on Lotus and it closed its doors in 1998.

LUC BERJEN

Founded in 1988 by the Anglo-French couple Jennifer Loss and Bernard Didelle, Luc Berjen shoes are designed in London and made in Italy. The company was vying for attention in the high-fashion luxury market but after 2006 it took a more mid-market approach to cope with the recession.

LUCCHESE

Italian-born Sam Lucchese founded the Lucchese Boot Company in San Antonio, Texas, in 1883. In 1960 his grandson, also named Sam, inherited the company and changed the lasts for making the boots, resulting in a better fitting product that gained a reputation for being one of the best cowboy boots around.

LUCIANO PADOVAN

A relative newcomer to the Italian fashion footwear scene, Luciano Padovan has a factory just outside Milan which produces around 500 pairs of shoes per day. Its shoes and handbags are sold through up-market stores in Milan, Rome, Moscow, Dubai and New York.

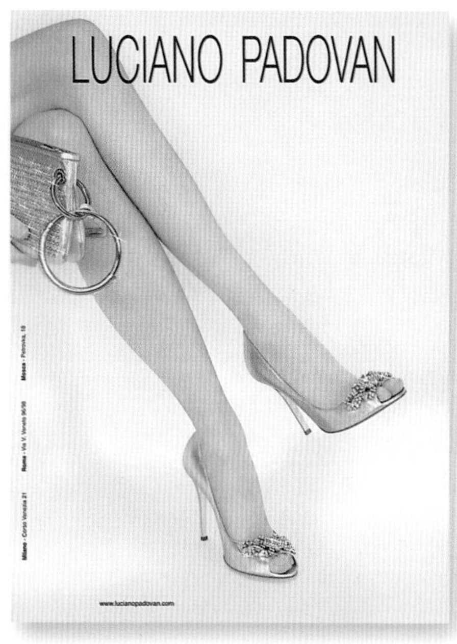

LUCIANO PADOVAN
Advertisement for Luciano Padovan, Autumn 2006

LUDWIG KOPP

One of Germany's first and largest shoe manufacturers, founded in 1857 by Hermann Schmidt and bought out by Ludwig Kopp in 1868. The company reached peak production in 1937; its best-known brand at the time was Elka. The company ceased production at the end of 1979.

LUDWIG REITER

Established in Vienna in 1885 by Ludwig Reiter, the company quickly grew to become known for the men's Goodyear-welted shoes that it still produces today. In 1934 Ludwig Reiter began making women's shoes under the brands Fox and Piccadilly. The company is now in its fourth generation of family operation and has seen its business expand since the 1990s. Women's shoes are now made under the label Anna Reiter.

LUICHINY

Spanish manufactured shoe brand created in 1982, known for following vintage revival trends.

LUICHINY
Heart motif leather boots with 9½-inch platforms, mid-1990s

MAERTENS, KLAUS *see* DOC MARTENS

MAGDESIANS
Low-heeled flat sandals in natural cork, late 2000s

MAGDESIANS

Line of mid-priced fashion comfort and casual shoes, made in California since 1952.

MAGLI, SANDRO

The son of **BRUNO MAGLI**, Sandro was apprenticed in his father's company and eventually became a partner. In 1990 he started his own company, Di Sandro, in Bologna, Italy, making high-fashion shoes and accessories.

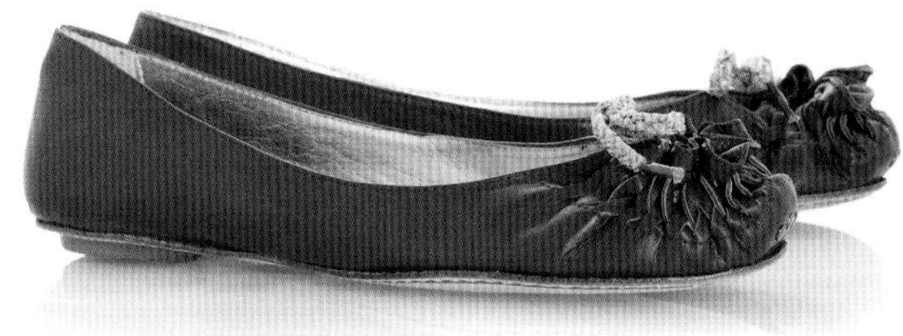

MALOLES ANTIGNAC
Leather ballet flats with gathered, round toes and cutout detail, in off-white patent leather and brown leather, late 2000s

MAGRIT

Magrit is a brand from one of the oldest Spanish shoe manufacturers still in existence. It was established in 1929 by José Amat Sanchez in the Alicante region of Spain. In 1940 Manuel, José's son, joined the company just as its export markets began to disappear, but by 1951 Magrit was exporting again, working with companies such as **BALLY**. It is now operated by the third generation of the Amat family, and 80 per cent of the Magrit shoes produced in Spain are exported, including its own brand and those made for Donna Karan, Bally, Carolina Herrera and L. K. Bennett.

MALOLES ANTIGNAC

Since launching her eponymous collection of ballerina flats in 2004, Antignac has expanded the French brand to include a full range of footwear, including heeled shoes and boots. Her luxury brand sells through prestigious stores from Tokyo to New York.

MANOLO BLAHNÍK

Blahník was born in 1942 in the Canary Islands. He studied literature and law in Geneva and art in Paris before moving to London in 1968. In 1971 Diana Vreeland, editor-in-chief of American *Vogue*, was impressed with his shoe designs, and he achieved his first critical success shortly after, when Ossie Clark invited him to make shoes for a runway show. Blahník began designing shoes for Zapata, a shop on Old Church Street in London, which he purchased in 1973 and which still remains his global headquarters. His American success came in 1978, when he launched a collection for Bloomingdales, and the following year he opened a store on Madison Avenue. In 1982 Blahník entered into a highly successful business partnership with George Malkemus and his American sales took off. In the 1980s Blahník created shoes for fashion designers Perry Ellis, Calvin Klein and Isaac Mizrahi. He opened a store in Hong Kong in 1991, and continued to collaborate with designers throughout the 1990s, including John Galliano, Bill Blass, Caroline Herrera and Oscar de la Renta. Blahník describes his stylish shoes as combining good quality with sex appeal. He is inspired by the work of **ROGER VIVIER**, but regards himself as a shoe artisan rather than a star designer. Blahník became a household name in the US thanks to the television series *Sex and the City*, in which Carrie Bradshaw (played by Sarah Jessica Parker) indulged her obsession for his shoes. In 2003 Blahník was the first shoe designer to have an exhibition at the London Design Museum.

MANOLO BLAHNIK
31 WEST 54TH ST NEW YORK • 49-51 OLD CHURCH ST LONDON • BERGDORF GOODMAN NEW YORK • NEIMAN MARCUS STORES • WYNN LAS VEGAS

MANOLO BLAHNÍK
Advertisement for Manolo Blahník, Autumn 2006

MANOLO BLAHNÍK
Leather sandals with flower-petal design, 2003

MANOLO BLAHNÍK
Embroidered purple silk mules, reissued in 2009 based on a design introduced in 1995

MANOLO BLAHNÍK
Below 'Caviara' design, cutout boot in silk piqué with grosgrain trim and satin lining on a painted stacked heel, Spring/Summer 2010

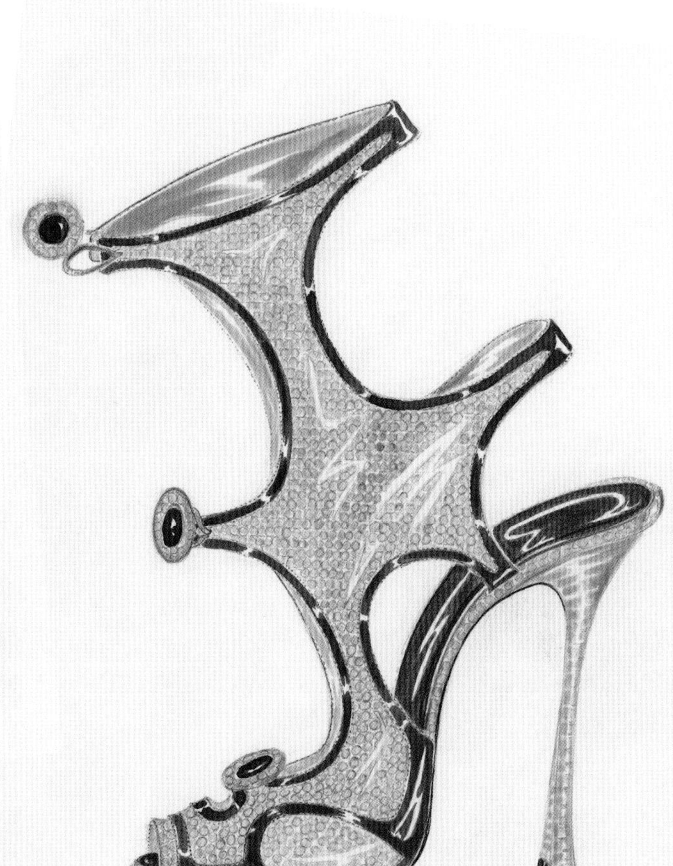

MANOLO BLAHNÍK
Above 'Ebete' design, open-toed slit bottine with side lacing and contrasting lining in satin or leather with painted edges, Spring/Summer 2010

MARANT

Founded in Montevideo, Uruguay, in the early 1960s by Martin Kollaian, the company specializes in women's high-fashion footwear using exotic leathers and hand-crafted finishing. Arika Nerguiz currently designs an eponymous ready-to-wear export line for Marant.

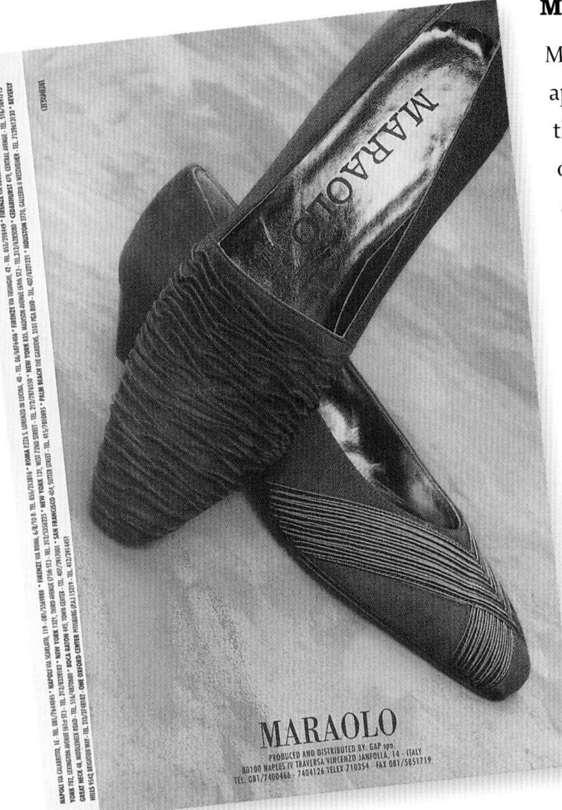

MARAOLO, MARIO

Maraolo was born in 1936, and was apprenticed to his father's tannery at the age of fifteen. Five years later he opened his own shoe factory in Naples, and by the mid-1960s he was opening stores in Europe and the US, carrying his brands Maraolo and Coca. In 1979 he started producing leather goods for both Giorgio Armani and the Emporio Armani. He also produces footwear for Donna Karan and Joan Halpern's **JOAN & DAVID** line. About 40 per cent of his company's daily production of nearly 3,000 pairs of shoes for men and women is exported to the US.

MARGARET JERROLD

After the Second World War Jerrold Miller started work in the shoe factory founded by his great-grandfather Israel Miller. His wife, Margaret Clark, had started as an in-house designer for **I. MILLER** in the 1940s, and in 1954 they created a line called Margaret Jerrold. In 1963 Margaret received a Neiman Marcus award for her sophisticated low-heeled designs. In 1964 Jerrold

MARAOLO, MARIO
Above **Advertisement for Mario Maraolo, Winter 1991**

Left **Advertisement for Mario Maraolo, Summer 1990**

MARGARET JERROLD
Taxi theme appliqué leather pumps, mid-1980s

Miller launched the Shoe Biz department at Henri Bendel in New York, carrying fashion lines from **WALTER STEIGER** among others. In the same year Miller established a wholesale business called Super Shoe Biz, which imported shoes from Italy and Spain, and later Southeast Asia. In 1978 Miller began phasing out the Margaret Jerrold brand in favour of imports, and officially changed the firm's name to Shoe Biz. The brand finally disappeared in 1989, when Miller retired. Clark and Miller had divorced in the 1960s and Margaret Clark died in 1994.

MARINO FABIANI

Company established in 1979 making high-fashion youthful, sexy footwear.

MARLOES TEN BHÖMER
Beige folded shoes, each made from a single piece of leather, with a stainless-steel heel construction, 2009

MARLOES TEN BHÖMER

Dutch-born artist and shoemaker Marloes ten Bhömer works out of London. Active only since 2003, she creates primarily deconstructivist shoes that blur the line between wearable art and avant-garde design.

MARY CLAUD

Founded by Massimi Luigi in 1954 in the Marche region of Italy, the company is now managed by his sons Stefano and Claudio. Using the best modern technology, the company produces high-fashion feminine footwear with an eye to comfort.

MASCARO

Established in Ferreries (Minorca), Spain, in 1918, Mascaro began as a workshop, hand-making ballet slippers. Under the direction of the founder's son, Jaime Mascaro, the company expanded into shoemaking and moved from handmade to factory production. In the 1980s Mascaro began opening stores, primarily in Spain, France and England. Third-generation Lina and Ursula Mascaro took over the company in the late 1990s and continue to expand its retail outlets around the world, including the US. Ursula has designed her eponymous brand since the late 1990s; the other Mascaro brands are Jaime Mascaro and Pretty Ballerinas.

MASSARO
Beige leather sling-back pumps with black patent toecaps, labelled Chanel, mid-1980s. Both Raymond Massaro and René Mancini took credit for creating this timeless design in 1957

MASSARO

Sebastien Massaro founded his shoemaking firm in 1894 at 2 rue de la Paix in Paris. The company was little known outside its exclusive circle of customers until it came under the direction of Sebastien's grandson Raymond, who joined the company in 1947. In 1957 Raymond designed the beige pump with black toecap and heel that became Chanel's trademark shoe design. The style has been in production ever since, as either a closed pump or a sling-back. In 1994 the French government awarded Raymond the title Master of Art for his consummate ability to produce finely crafted footwear. He continues to create custom shoe designs for a long list of clients and clothing designers, and oversees designs at Massaro, which was bought by Chanel in 2002.

MAUD FRIZON
Left Navy blue and silver kid D'Orsay pumps, mid-1980s

Below Advertisement for Maud Frizon, Autumn 1979

MAUD FRIZON

Nadine Frizon was born in 1941, and changed her name to Maud when she began modelling for Parisian couturiers, including Jean Patou and André Courrèges. In the 1960s models were expected to use their own shoes on assignments; unable to find shoes she wanted, Frizon decided to make her own. She and her husband, Gigi de Marco, opened a shop on rue des Saints-Pères on the Left Bank in Paris, where Frizon presented her first collection in 1969, featuring an iconic zipless tall boot design. The line was an instant success, taken up by stars such as Brigitte Bardot. Frizon was a leading shoe designer in the 1980s,

MAUD FRIZON
Multi-coloured snakeskin sandals, early 1980s

when she created the cone heel and designed for Azzedine Alaïa, Claude Montana, Thierry Mugler and Sonia Rykiel. Frizon sold her company, and her name, in 1999. In 1993 Frizon de Marco opened Ombeline brand shops in Paris, St Tropez and New York; each season she creates new styles, which are known for their mixing of colours and materials.

MAURIZIO CELIN *see* **CONSOLIDATED SHOE**

MAX KIBARDIN

Born in Siberia and educated in Italy, Max Kibardin launched his own brand in 2004. His shoes reflect his training and interest in minimalist architecture and engineering.

MEISI

Fritz Keyl founded his eponymous company in Radebeul, Germany, in 1916. Rebuilt in Rintein after the Second World War, the company continued to be run by the founder until his death in 1963. The company, renamed Meisi by its new owner, Heinrich Siegmann, concentrated on comfort footwear, a speciality of the German footwear industry.

MELISSA *see* **GRENDENE**

MELVILLE *see* **THOM McAN**

MAX KIBARDIN
High-heeled leather pumps in black and red leather, both Spring/Summer 2010

MAX KIBARDIN

Above Multi-coloured satin stiletto heel, Spring/Summer 2010

Above right Open-toed ankle boot in purple leather with stiletto heel and covered platform, Spring/Summer 2010

Right Purple satin high-heeled sandal, Spring/Summer 2010

MEPHISTO
Leather sandals with contoured footbeds, 2009

MEPHISTO

Martin Michaeli established Mephisto in 1965 in France, with the goal of creating comfortable and stylish shoes. The brand was being distributed throughout Europe by the late 1960s, and expanded to Japan and North America in the 1980s. In 1999 French retailers selected Mephisto as the best French footwear brand, and in 2000 Michaeli was made a member of the French Légion d'honneur. Mephisto also manufactures the brands Mobils, Sano and Allrounder, and now has sales in over sixty countries.

MERRELL

Manufacturer founded in 1981 by Clark Matis, John Schweitzer and Randy Merrell, with the goal to improve the fit and comfort of recreational outdoor footwear. Innovations included hiking boots with narrower heels and air-cushioned soles. The company was bought out by **WOLVERINE** in 1997 and has grown to dominate the 'aftersport' casual market, combining the comfort and fit of sports shoes with dressier styles.

MICHEL PERRY

Above **Platform sandals, Autumn/Winter 2009**

Above right **Ankle boots with cuff and back strap, Autumn/Winter 2009**

MICHEL PERRY

Born in 1949, Perry studied painting in Belgium before he was apprenticed with an independent bootmaker in France. He created his first self-named collection in 1987 and quickly followed by opening a boutique near Les Halles in Paris. Perry designed his first men's footwear collection in 2001, and in 2004 opened a flagship store on rue Saint-Honoré. In 2007 the first Michel Perry Collector concept store opened in Paris.

MINNA PARIKKA
Opposite Suede and metallic leather shoes, Autumn/Winter 2009

MINNETONKA MOCCASIN
Below Fringed mid-height suede boot with leather laces, tassel and bead accents, late 2000s

Below right Fringed short suede boot with a back zip, late 2000s

MICHEL VIVIEN

Born in Grenoble in 1962, Michel Vivien moved to Paris in 1982 to study art. He has worked as a freelance shoe designer since 1990, creating collections for **MICHEL PERRY**, **CHARLES JOURDAN**, **SERGIO ROSSI**, **CASADEI**, Alexander McQueen for Givenchy, Galliano for Dior, and for Yves Saint Laurent's last three haute couture collections. In 1998 Vivien launched his own label but went on to become the artistic director for Robert **CLERGERIE**. In 2006 he began designing the shoe collections for Alber Elbaz for Lanvin.

MIHARA YASUHIRO

After graduating from Tama Art University in Tokyo, Mihara Yasuhiro took on a short shoemaking apprenticeship before launching his eponymous brand of shoes in 1998. He specializes in manipulating leather into a rumpled, used look that has been called 'post-apocalyptic urban' style. In 2000 he began a collaboration with Puma but his 'preworn' aesthetic is reserved for his own collection.

MINNA PARIKKA

Finnish-born Minna Parikka launched her eponymous brand in 2005. Her flagship boutique in Helsinki showcases her vintage-inspired collection of shoes and boots that also exhibit a hint of fetish chic.

MINNETONKA MOCCASIN

Founded in 1946 by Philip Miller, Minnetonka became a huge success in the late 1960s and early 1970s, when their Native American fringed leather styling appealed to the hippie generation. Driving mocs and beaded slippers have kept the company in business during the lean times but whenever the trend for Native-style boots and mocs is revived, Minnetonka is there.

TRACEY NEULS

Left Black and red oxfords that reflect Neuls's interest in textile, surface and sculptural form, Autumn/Winter 2009

Below left Black leather lace-up boots with sculptural colour-contrast heel, Autumn/Winter 2009

MODA RUGGI *see* APEPAZZA

MORESCHI

Founded in 1946 in Vigevano, Italy, the company of over 300 employees now manufactures over 240,000 pairs of fashion boots shoes per year. Besides footwear, Moreschi also produces accessories, clothing and leather goods.

NATURALIZER

see BROWN SHOE COMPANY

NEULS, TRACEY

Canadian-born Tracey Neuls trained at Cordwainers College, London, before launching her own company, TN_29, in 2000. Her organically shaped heels and uppers were fresh concepts and found critical acclaim. Neuls opened a TN_29 boutique in London in 2005.

NEWTON ELKIN

Frequently referred to as an influential American shoe designer of the twentieth century, Newton Elkin is an obscure figure. From his home town in Philadelphia he produced designs for a number of brands, which usually gave him joint credit. He was most famous for Pandora, available from the 1930s until the 1960s. In 1937 he was the first designer to put zipper closures on fashion shoes. Advertisements for shoes with his name can be found until the late 1970s, when it is thought he died.

TRACEY NEULS
Opposite **Shoes employing reissued vintage textiles from the iconic British textiles company Sanderson, Spring/Summer 2010**

NEWTON ELKIN
Right **Advertisement for Newton Elkin, Autumn 1952**

Shadow sandals by Newton Elkin
A lace face shows through clear vinylite— the romantic picture framed in black-of-night suede. Sling or ankle strap, medium or high heel, 23.95 On the Fourth Floor, Lord & Taylor

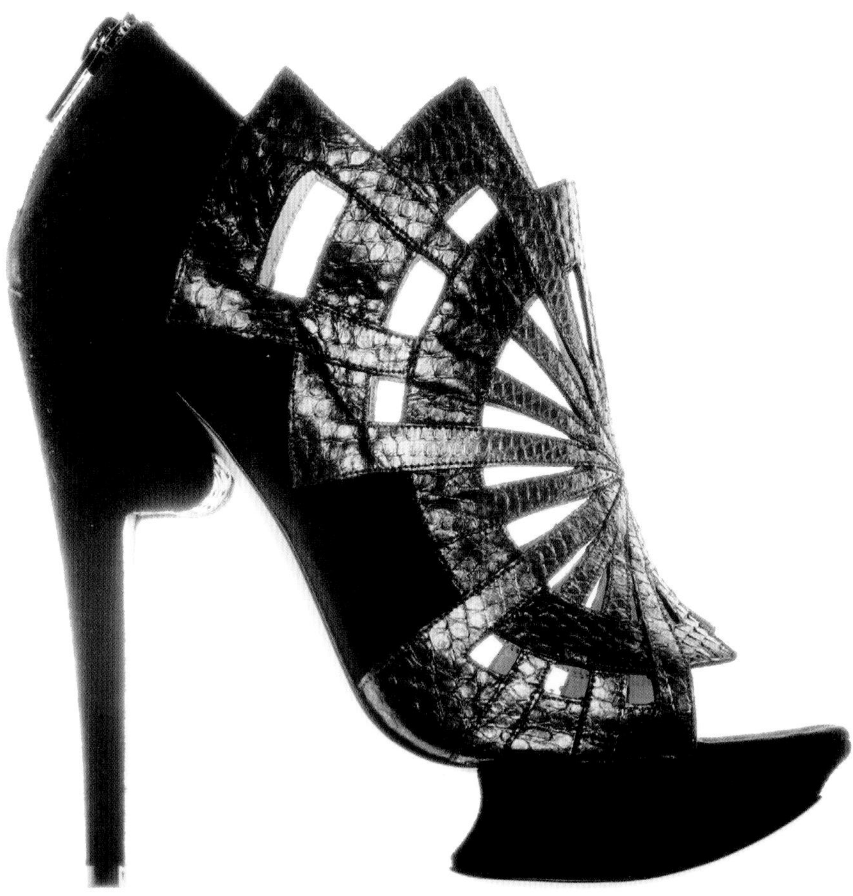

NICHOLAS KIRKWOOD

Born in 1978, this British designer attended Cordwainers College before launching his eponymous line of shoes in 2005. His feminine yet conspicuously contemporary shoes are inspired by architecture and use exotic materials, while avoiding obvious historical references. With half a dozen other designers Kirkwood is leading the way in women's high-fashion footwear of the twenty-first century. Aside from his own collection Kirkwood has designed shoes for Chloé, Phillip Lim and Zac Posen, among others.

NICHOLAS KIRKWOOD
Black, bronze and gold snakeskin platform stiletto shoe with back zip, Autumn/Winter 2009

NICOLE BRUNDAGE

Born in San Antonio, Texas, Nicole graduated in Fine Arts from Stanford University before attending the Istituto Marangoni in Milan, where she studied fashion design. After an internship at Giorgio Armani she worked with **MANOLO BLAHNÍK**, before heading to New York to design the 2004 shoe collection for Zac Posen. She launched her own line of shoes in 2006 and has collaborated with many other established labels, including **SALVATORE FERRAGAMO** and Max Mara. Her shoes are heavily influenced by vintage fetish imagery.

NICOLE BRUNDAGE
Below 'Yoko' red suede sandal, Spring/Summer 2010

Below right 'Yokona' green suede sandal, Spring/Summer 2010

NICOLE BRUNDAGE
Below **'Urika Celeste' open-toed leather ankle boot, Spring/Summer 2010**

Opposite above **'Twila' sandal from the Acrobats of God Collection by Nicole Brundage, Spring/Summer 2010**

Opposite below left **'Eden' cream and black leather sandal, Spring/Summer 2010**

Opposite below right **'Loui' black sandal in patent leather and suede with pom-pom detail, Spring/Summer 2010**

NINA

In 1953 Stanley and Mike Silverstein began their shoe careers tacking basic leather uppers to wood soles in the small clog-making shop founded by their father, a Cuban émigré. In 1962 they started Nina in a small SoHo loft in New York City. Nina had grown very successful by the late 1960s, through a series of expansions and profitable purchases of Spanish boot exports. The brothers remained in charge of the company: Stanley was in charge of design and manufacturing, while Mike dealt with sales. The company presently manufactures the lines Nina, Touch of Nina, Nina Doll and Elements by Nina; it also acquired the redundant Delman label (*see* **HERMAN DELMAN**) to build a luxury footwear line.

NINE WEST

Jerome Fisher and Vincent Camuto founded a wholesale shoe business called Fisher Camuto in 1977. Each had a background in the shoe business: Fisher had gone from working in the family's shoe factory to opening his own in 1958; Camuto had worked for Japanese importer Sumitomo Corporation of America, where he developed marketing and distribution plans. Their company imported shoes from Brazilian manufacturers under the name Nine West, their first address on 57th Street in Manhattan. They started a sister company called Jervin (formed by joining their first names) in 1988 to supply retailers with unbranded Brazilian-made women's shoes. Fisher Camuto was designer-savvy and quick with its production of moderate-priced footwear. The sister companies merged in 1993 to form Nine West, which was successful enough to buy out American shoemaking giant **UNITED STATES SHOE CORPORATION** in 1995. It closed down much of US Shoe's operations and moved production to Brazil. In 1999 clothing manufacturer and distributor **JONES APPAREL GROUP** bought Nine West for $1.4 billion and quickly integrated it into its own company.

NINA
Red satin sandals from the holiday collection, 2009

NINE WEST
Advertisement for Nine West, Spring 1998

NINA
Silver and purple peep-toe sequin pumps
from the holiday collection, 2009

PACO GIL

Above Black net and kid piping on patent-leather wedge heel with back zipper enclosure, 2009–10

Left Royal-blue crinkle patent leather with silver electroplated heel and multiple buckles, Summer 2008

NUSRALA SHOE COMPANY

Founded in St. Louis, the company is known for brands such as Da Venci and La Pattie. Nusrala was sold in 1964, becoming a part of the St. Louis **CONSOLIDATED SHOE COMPANY**.

NUSRALA SHOE COMPANY
Advertisement for LaPatti brand of shoes by Nusrala Shoe Company, Autumn 1961

OFFICE

Shoe retailer Office London opened in 1981 as a footwear concession in the chic London shop Hyper Hyper. The first Office store opened on Kings Road in 1984. The company has expanded to include over a hundred stand-alone stores and concessions around the UK under its own name, as well as Offspring, Poste and Poste Mistress.

OTWAY, FLORENCE

Florence Otway's career began as an illustrator in the early 1940s, but quickly turned to design. Like many shoe designers, she worked anonymously under other labels, in her case almost every major luxury New York footwear brand: **I. MILLER** (1943), **PALIZZIO** (1950), **GENESCO** (Mademoiselle line, 1954–57 and 1960–68), Caressa (1957–60), **DAVID EVINS** (1968), **GAROLINI** (1974), **GOLO** (1976; she was the first shoe designer to use Gore-Tex for boots), Calvin Klein (1984), Adrienne Vittadini (1989), as well as freelance work for **GUCCI**, **BERNARDO** and **BALLY**. She retired in 1991.

PACIOTTI *see* **CESARE PACIOTTI**

PACO GIL

Shoe designer Paco Gil created his eponymous brand in 1982. The shoes are made in Elda, Alicante, Spain, for domestic sale and export around the world. They are known for cutting-edge high-fashion footwear.

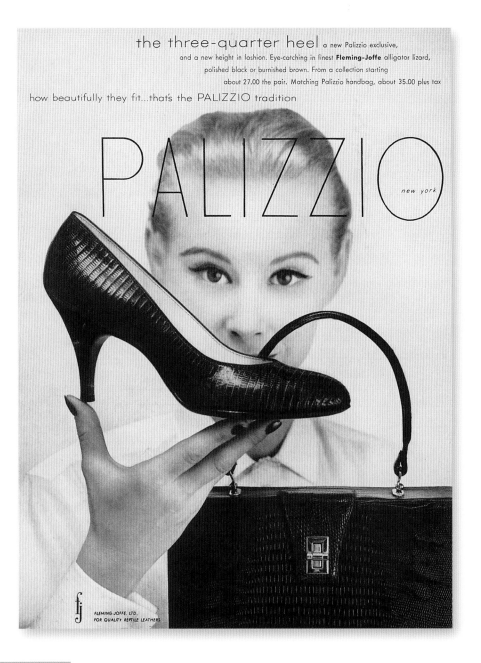

the three-quarter heel a new Palizzio exclusive, and a new height in fashion. Eye-catching in finest **Fleming-Joffe** alligator lizard, polished black or burnished brown. From a collection starting about 27.00 the pair. Matching Palizzio handbag, about 35.00 plus tax

how beautifully they fit...that's the PALIZZIO tradition

PALIZZIO

new york

fj

FLEMING-JOFFE, LTD.
FOR QUALITY REPTILE LEATHERS

PALIZZIO

Above Advertisement for Palizzio, Summer 1964

Left Advertisement for Palizzio, Summer 1956

PALIZZIO
Brown leather, brocade and lamé shoes, *c.* 1970

PALIZZIO

Palizzio was founded as a family company around 1950 by Leo Gordon, as an offshoot of Thomas Cort Shoes, established by his brother Reuben. Leo's grandson Michael Abrams joined the company in 1967, and took it over in 1980; he opened factories in Spain and Italy to produce the brands Palizzio, Proxy and Perry Ellis. In 1988 Arcadia International Shoe Corporation bought Palizzio, but Abrams continued in the industry, founding Kasper Footwear in 1995. Palizzio shoes were always good at balancing practical style with high-fashion colours and details.

PALTER DE LISO

Daniel Palter founded a shoe company in New York in 1919, and in 1927 joined with James DeLiso. Palter was the businessman, DeLiso the designer. The company promoted coloured-leather shoes in the 1930s and received a Neiman Marcus award in 1938 for introducing open-toed, sling-back pumps, which were originally deemed controversial. In the 1950s the De Liso Debs line, for which Mabel **JULIANELLI** created designs, was added for a younger audience. Palter's son Richard took over the company until it closed in 1975.

PALTER DE LISO

Above Advertisement for De Liso Debs, Winter 1951–52

Left Fuchsia suede and gold kid platform shoes, *c.* 1950

PANCALDI

Four generations of the family have overseen Pancaldi since Natale Pancaldi crafted his first shoe in Bologna in 1888. The main expansion came after the Second World War under the founder's grandson, Natalino. He modernized the company and increased its exports. Stefano Pancaldi currently presides over the company, most of whose production is now exported. Pancaldi has made shoes for **MANOLO BLAHNÍK**, **WALTER STEIGER**, Isaac Mizrahi, Fausto Santini and **PHILIPPE MODEL**. In 1986 the company was licensed to produce footwear for Escada.

PAPPAGALLOS *see* **ENCORE SHOE CORPORATION**

PALTER DE LISO
Advertisment for De Liso Debs, Autumn 1956

PANCALDI
Advertisement for Pancaldi for Delman, Autumn 1985

PATRICK COX

Cox was born in Edmonton, Canada, in 1963. In the early 1980s he worked in Toronto for fashion designer Loucas Kleanthous, who recognized his talent and encouraged him to study at Cordwainers College in London. Success came quickly and within a year of starting college Cox was designing platform shoes for Vivienne Westwood's 1984 Witches collection. Soon he was designing footwear for John Galliano, Workers for Freedom and Anna Sui, and as early as 1985 he was able to set up his own company. A private label collection followed in 1987, made first in England then later in Italy. The first Patrick Cox shop opened in 1991 in London, where he sold classic looks and revisited favourites. There are now stores in Paris and New York. Cox's most successful design has been the 1993 Wannabe loafer, a colourful revival of the classic hush-puppies style. Between 2003 and 2005 he was head of design for **CHARLES JOURDAN**.

PATRICK COX
Gold leather sandals with platform wedge heels decorated with chandeliers, 2005

PEDRO GARCIA

Pedro Garcia founded a children's shoemaking workshop in Elda, Alicante, Spain, in 1925, soon transforming it into a factory making men's footwear. In 1954 his son, also called Pedro, took over the company and began specializing in women's footwear. A new factory was opened in 1965 and in 1968 Pedro Garcia shoes were being sold at Henri Bendel and Bergdorf Goodman in New York, and Russell & Bromley stores in the UK. The third Pedro Garcia and his sister Mila are now in charge, with Pedro looking after design and Mila anaging the company. The high-fashion footwear is sold in stores and online.

PEGABO *see* **ALDO**

PATRICK COX
Above Advertisement for Patrick Cox, Spring 1997

Right Green jellies with metal Big Ben ornament inside water-filled heels, Summer 1996

PENALJO

Founded in the late 1930s in St. Louis, Missouri, by Penn Hamilton, the company specialized in walking shoes and stylish low-heeled casuals. It was bought out from bankruptcy protection in 1990 and revived as a comfort brand by Norwood Shoe Corporation.

PETER FOX

Peter Fox was born in London, England, and attended Camberwell Art School in London and Maidstone Art School in Kent, where he studied sculpture. After a stint at retail in Harrods department store in London he moved to Vancouver, Canada, in 1956, where he was offered a job selling shoes. In 1970 he went into partnership with **JOHN FLUEVOG**, opening a shop that specialized in edgy, youthful designs. Fox met his wife, Linda, in the store while she was shopping for boots, and in 1981 the two opened Peter Fox Shoes in SoHo, New York. Together they designed shoes which combined strong historical references with a prescience for trends, such as the granny boot collection of 1982, Louis-heeled pumps in 1985, and platforms in 1986 (all of them a couple of years before their popular return). Peter Fox also made footwear for Broadway productions. In 2007 Peter Fox closed his shop in New York and retired. Helga Magi, who had been his SoHo store manager, took on the business and continues to have Peter Fox shoes made in Italy for online sales.

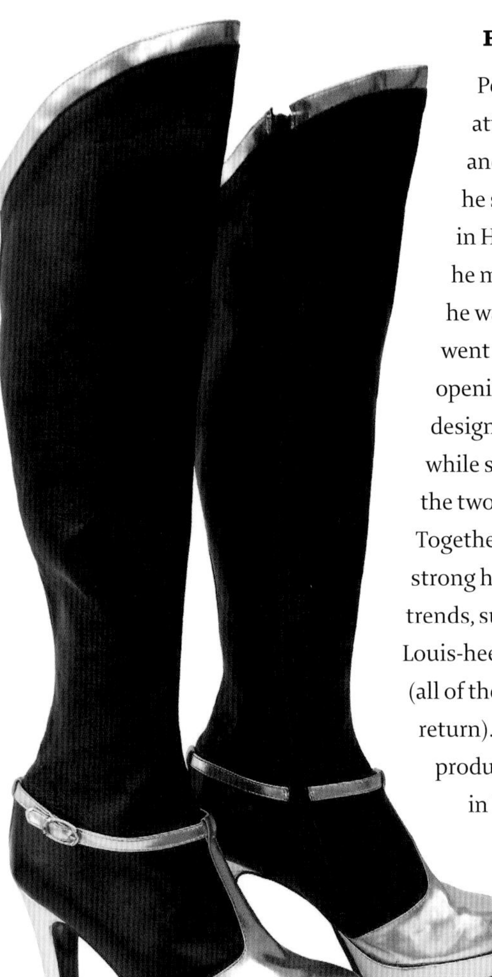

PENALJO
Advertisement for Penaljo, Spring 1951

PETER FOX
Black and gold leather boots made in Spain for Fox and Fluevog, 1977

PETER KAISER
Green leather and snakeskin platform shoes, Paradies brand by Peter Kaiser, early 1970s

PETER FOX
Leather boot inspired by stained glass, 1973

PETER KAISER

Peter Kaiser established a shoemaker's shop in 1838 in Pirmasens, Germany, and became one of the country's first industrial shoe manufacturers, establishing the town as the seat of the German shoe industry. The company specializes in women's high-fashion footwear and produces about a million pairs of shoes per year in Germany and at its sister plant in Portugal.

PHILIPPE MODEL

French designer Philippe Model is an innovator in the use of elastic materials in shoes. In 1983 he made a simple flat shoe using heavy lingerie elastic for the upper. This simple design concept has been carried over into a wide range of boots, pumps and mules.

PIERRE HARDY

Hardy was born in 1956 and attended the Ecole Nationale Supérieure des Beaux-Arts in Paris. He began designing shoes for Dior in 1988 and Hermès in 1990, and launched his own line in 1998. He is famous for his 'blade' heel, a thin rectangle that looks like a stiletto heel from the side and a block heel from the back. Hardy also designs a line of fashion sneakers and has been designing a shoe collection for Gap since 2005.

PONS QUINTANA

Founded in 1953 by Santiago Pons Quintana in the village of Alaior (Minorca), Spain, this company is known for its woven leather shoes and sandals.

POUR LA VICTOIRE

Brand designed by David Giordano in New York starting about 2007, the high-fashion shoes are made in Brazil.

PUPI D'ANGIERI

The Italian company located in Parabiago, Italy, began in women's fashion footwear, but expanded in the early 1990s to include a men's line, a comfort line called Boxes, sportswear under the brand Max Frey, a Brazilian-made label called Pupi, and Natalie Acatrini, a high-end salon line. In 1992 it acquired the licence for Donna Karan shoes.

PUPI D'ANGIERI
Advertisement for Pupi D'Angieri, Winter 1986

PIERRE HARDY
Top **Metallic soft nappa sling-back pumps, late 2000s**

Above **Black patent peep-toe pumps with stiletto heels, late 2000s**

PURA LOPEZ

Spanish shoe company founded in 1956 by Antonio Lopez Moreno; Pura Lopez is now designing for the family business a line of mid-price high-fashion footwear basics.

QUALICRAFT

American brand of affordable women's shoes, established around 1950. The shoes were sold through the Bakers-Leeds chain in the United States, but the company supplied independent and department stores at home and abroad until its demise in 1980.

QUEEN QUALITY

The company grew out of a brand of that name established by Thomas Plant in 1898. After the Second World War Queen Quality's factory in Jamaica Plains, Massachusetts, was the largest factory in the world making only women's shoes. The shoes were of high quality but reasonably priced. Production ceased in the 1960s and in 1976 the empty building burned.

R. GIGGS *see* DOC MARTENS

RAUTUREAU

In 1870 Jean-Baptiste Rautureau established a shoemaking workshop in La Gaubretière, France, from where his grandsons, designer Guy and his brother Yvon, continue to produce footwear. Their brand,

QUALICRAFT
Advertisement for Qualicraft brand shoes sold at Bakers-Leeds, Autumn 1974

QUEEN QUALITY
Advertisement for Queen Quality brand shoes by International Shoe Company, Autumn 1960

Apple Shoes, was founded in 1975 to appeal to a hip, young market with lines such as Pom D'Api, Free Lance, Slugger, Etnies (skateboard shoes), Spring Court and No Name. They became known in the 1990s for their chic platforms and also for their creative packaging, replacing the standard cardboard shoebox for corrugated plastic and tin-plate boxes painted by Loulou Picasso. Their shoes sell from a worldwide chain of Free Lance stores.

RAYNE *see* **H. & R. RAYNE**

REBECA SANVER

Jose Juan Sanchis Busquier founded the manufacturer Florencia Marco in 1987 in Elda, Spain. Though it is still officially listed under that name, it is popularly known by its trademark collection of ladies' footwear, Rebeca Sanver. In 2003 the company launched To Be, a youthful, affordable brand.

RED CROSS

From 1905 until the 1960s Red Cross was a popular brand of shoe, known for its bendable comfort sole. In 1942 the company agreed to suspend the use of the name so as not to be in conflict with the humanitarian organization. The shoes were made originally in Cincinnati by Krohn Fechheimer, one of the companies that became the **UNITED STATES SHOE CORPORATION**.

RED OR DEAD

Wayne and Geraldine Hemingway began a vintage clothing stall in Camden Market in 1982, at first producing street-style fashions and a year later popularizing **DOC MARTENS** boots. Red or Dead eventually opened shops around England and as far away as Copenhagen and Tokyo. It won Street Style Designer of the Year awards from the British Fashion Council in 1995, 1996 and 1997. It was bought out by Pentland Brand in 1996.

RED OR DEAD
Boots from the Space Baby collection designed by Red or Dead for Doc Martens, Spring/Summer 1990

SPACE BABY
"DON'T WORRY ABOUT THE FUTURE
YOU ARE IN SAFE HANDS"
RED OR DEAD
SPRING SUMMER COLLECTION 1990

RENÉ CAOVILLA

René Caovilla was apprenticed in his father's shoemaking business in the Riviera del Brenta near Venice in 1952, and in 1955 he created his first collection. Caovilla has always emphasized quality over quantity, and began selling his shoes – renowned for their embroidery and inlays – to an exclusive clientele from all over Europe. In the 1980s he collaborated with Yves Saint Laurent and by the end of the 1990s he was producing shoes for Chanel and Dior. He opened his first boutique in Venice in 2000 and has continued expanding into foreign markets.

RENÉ CAOVILLA
Black suede evening shoes with wired ankle straps, early 1990s

RENÉ MANCINI
Dark navy leather pumps made by René Mancini for Lauren Bacall, late 1960s

RENÉ MANCINI

René Mancini was one of the remaining Parisian shoemakers who provided superb handmade, bespoke shoes for the clients of couturiers Balmain, Givenchy, Manguin, Fath and Chanel. He began his career in 1953 and included in his list of clients Jacqueline Kennedy, Greta Garbo, Princess Grace, Queen Sirikit of Thailand, Lauren Bacall and Audrey Hepburn. The company continued after his death in 1986.

RIEKER

Heinrich Rieker established the Rieker Shoe Company in Tutlingen, Germany, in 1874. The company, which produces casual and fashion comfort footwear, expanded into the United States in 1986, Great Britain in 1990 with the purchase of Brevitt, and into Canada in 1995. Rieker has factories in Eastern Europe, North Africa and Vietnam, producing over 70,000 pairs of shoes per day, for export to over fifty countries.

ROBERT CLERGERIE
Fashion shots of shoes, Winter 2006

ROBERT CLERGERIE

Clergerie was an army officer, an accountant and an estate agent before he studied at the Ecole Supérieure de Commerce in Paris. On the strength of his evidently persuasive authority, rather than on any design background, he became an executive with **CHARLES JOURDAN** in 1970, and ran its Xavier Danaud subsidiary. In 1978 Clergerie acquired a controlling interest in the **UNIC** shoe company in Romans, France, restructured it, and designed and launched a self-named brand in 1981. In 1983 he launched a men's line, called Joseph Fenestrier after the founder of Unic. Clergerie's unornamented and clean designs won him *Footwear News* Designer of the Year awards in 1987 and 1990. The Fashion Footwear Association of New York awarded him in 1992 for his architecturally designed heels. Clergerie expanded to include a less expensive line of shoes called Espace by Robert Clergerie. He retired in 1996, but in 2005 bought back his eponymous company, participating in development of the collections. In 2005 Clergerie was entered into the Fashion Footwear Association Hall of Fame.

ROBERTO BOTTICELLI

High-fashion Italian brand founded in 1941 with its showroom in Milan. The company excels at making updated classic styles: fashionable though not trendy.

ROCKPORT

The brand Rockport was created in 1973 when Bruce Katz, working for his father's import business in Boston, saw that among the shoes in plain white boxes was a line of casual dress shoes made from leather which was called Rockport. He printed the name Rockport on the boxes creating the brand name. It became very popular by the early 1980s. Reebok acquired Rockport in 1986, and Adidas acquired Reebok and all its holdings in 2005.

ROBERT CLERGERIE
Black kid platform shoes, mid-1990s

RODOLPHE MENUDIER

Rodolphe worked as a freelance shoe designer for many French couture houses before starting his own label in Paris in 1994. In 1996 he began a line of men's shoes and in 2001 opened his own boutique on rue Castiglione in Paris.

ROGER VIVIER

Roger Vivier (1907–98) studied sculpture at the Ecole des Beaux-Arts in Paris. In 1937 he opened his first atelier on the rue Royale and was soon working as a freelance designer for various manufacturers, including Pinet, **BALLY** and **HERBERT DELMAN**. Vivier worked in New York in the early 1940s, where he studied millinery and in 1945 opened a hat shop with Suzanne Remy called Suzanne & Roger. Vivier returned to Paris in 1947 and found freelance work, including designing Queen Elizabeth II's coronation shoes in 1953. Later that year he created a line of prêt-à-porter shoes under the Delman–Christian Dior label. In 1955 he became the first shoe designer to have his name featured alongside that of a couturier when his designs carried the label 'Christian Dior créé par Roger Vivier' (Dior created by Vivier). While with Dior and his successor, Yves Saint Laurent, Vivier became renowned for the innovative designs of toes and heels. For Dior he created various stilettos, while for Laurent he created the 'comma' heel, in 1962, the first of several designs named after their shape; others included the ball, needle, pyramid, escargot and spool. In 1961 Vivier received a Neiman Marcus award, and in 1963 he opened his own design studio on the rue François 1er in Paris and created his signature line. Until 1972 he was a central figure in Paris couture, creating for Yves Saint Laurent, Emanuel Ungaro, Chanel and Hermès. His designs featured unusual materials, such as vinyl, metallic-finished leather, faux fur and stretch fabrics. In 1972 Vivier reduced his workload, taking on some design contracts but creating no new collections. An agreement with **RAUTUREAU APPLE SHOES** in 1994 to revive styles from his past collections brought Vivier out of his semi-retirement. Designs such as the comma and choc heels appeared again. In 1995 Vivier opened an eponymous Paris boutique, where he worked until his death in 1998. After his death, **DIEGO DELLA VALLE** acquired the company.

ROGER VIVIER
Above **Silver metallic evening pumps, mid-1960s**

Left **Black satin evening sandal with rhinestone orb heel, mid-1990s**

Opposite **Embroidered satin evening pumps, c. 1963**

ROSA SHOES
Left and below **Ankle-strap pump and oxford, 2009**

ROMIKA

Hellmuth Lemm acquired the Romika trademark from its founders in 1936, and by the 1950s it had become known for its rubber boots and rubber-soled shoes. The company moved into the casual shoe market, and expanded production into Spain in the 1960s and 1970s. After Hellmuth Lemm died in 1988 Romika was sold to Rene Jaeggi, who resold the company to **JOSEF SEIBEL** in 2005. Today the production of five million pairs per year is based in Eastern Europe and the Far East.

ROOTS

Michael Budman and Don Green were inspired by the early 1970s health shoe trend (from **BIRKENSTOCK** and **EARTH SHOES** for example) and in 1973 they began a small manufacturer and retailer in Toronto, Canada, called Roots. Today Roots has expanded into clothing and accessories and is sold through more than 120 retail locations in Canada and the United States, and over sixty more in Asia.

Roots Mule
Made from soft, Nubuck leather, this sophisticated, European look is great for evening or day wear.
$79.95
Roots Corkees
Authentic cork platform sole, environmental vegetable tanned leather, lightweight, attractive and fun.
$69.95
Evening Sandal
Soft suede straps, vegetable tanned leather inner sole and a natural rubber outer sole.
$39.95
All Terrain Sandal
ade with a Nubuck leather top, adjustable velcro strap,
brass rivet for reinforcement, a textured grip sole,
eoprene insole, blown rubber outsole
nd arch support.
59.95
Fisherman Sandal
Genuine, full-grain leather, durable rubber Roots sole for comfort, stitched leather welt construction and a nickel buckle.
$95.00
fresh Roots
BEAUTIFUL, COMFORTABLE, NEW
& MADE IN CANADA
The natural place to shop for shoes, since 1973.
Toronto • Montreal • Vancouver • Banff • Los Angeles • Chicago • Detroit
Roots

ROOTS
Advertisement for Roots shoes, Spring 1993

ROSA SHOES

RoSa Shoes began in the summer of 1983 when Roger and Sarah Adams began selling vintage stiletto-heeled shoes and English-made 'alternative styles', with exceedingly long, pointed toes, to followers of the punk and New Wave scenes. Continuing an extreme version of the winkle-picker style, RoSa shoes are now made in Italy, under the supervision of Edoardo Amaranti.

ROSINA FERRAGAMO SCHIAVONE

Sister of **SALVATORE FERRAGAMO**, Rosina designed shoes from the late 1960s into the 1980s. The lack of reference to Rosina's work by the Ferragamo company suggests her shoe designs were not wholly embraced by the Ferragamo family.

ROSINA FERRAGAMO SCHIAVONE
Above left **Black kid and brushed metal pumps, late 1960s**

Above **Beige, white and black patent leather sling-back pumps, late 1960s**

ROSSIMODA
Red patent leather shoe, *c.* 1970

ROSSIMODA

Narciso Rossi founded Rossimoda in Vigonza in 1942 as a family business, and it has been under his son Luigi's direction since 1956. It grew to become one of the largest manufacturers of high-end footwear, working under many labels: Yves Saint Laurent, Anne Klein, Ungaro and Genny, and more recently Lacroix, Givenchy, Pucci, Marc Jacobs, Kenzo, Celine, Donna Karan. In 2003 the LVMH Fashion Group assumed a controlling share of Rossimoda.

RUDOLF SCHEER

A shoemaking company for almost two hundred years (it was once official court shoemaker to Emperor Franz Joseph), Rudolf Scheer produces bespoke footwear. Though they never follow trends, the shoes are always of the finest quality. The company guarantees complimentary repair and service for as long as their original owners retain the shoes.

RUPERT SANDERSON

Born in 1966, Sanderson worked for **SERGIO ROSSI** before attending Cordwainers College in London between 1998 and 2000. He works from London and Bologna, and since 2001 has designed his own line of shoes, each of which is named after a variety of daffodil. He has also designed for Margaret Howell and Jean Muir. Sanderson's first store opened in Mayfair, London, in 2004.

RUDOLF SCHEER
Green suede pumps, late 1950s

RUPERT SANDERSON
Above 'Magnolia' navy suede pumps, Autumn/Winter 2009

Right 'Asteroid' black calf shoes, Autumn/Winter 2009

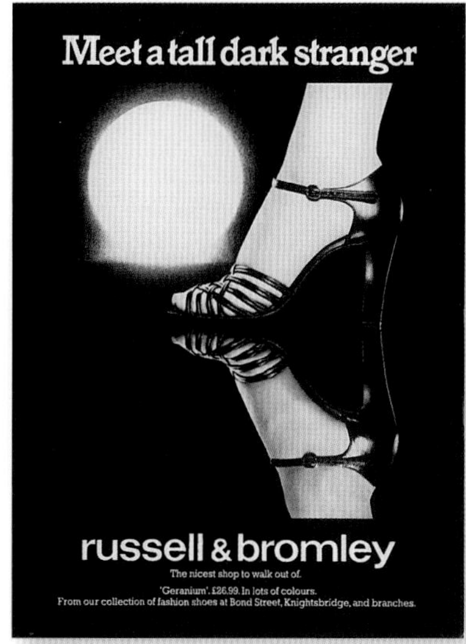

RUSSELL & BROMLEY

Though a retail company had been founded by John Russell in 1820, it was not until 1947 that the name Russell & Bromley emerged to become associated with high-street shoe stores. From its first shop, on the corner of Bond Street and Conduit Street, London, the chain had grown to forty-seven branches by 2009.

RUTHIE DAVIS

Davis began her career in footwear at Reebok, eventually becoming director of the Reebok Classics Division. After moving to marketing positions with Ugg and Tommy Hilfiger, Davis launched her own brand of contemporary high-fashion Italian-made shoes in 2006.

SACHA

A family-owned manufacturer in the Netherlands and founded in 1909 by Bart Termeer. His grandsons Bert and Paul took over the business in the 1970s and opened the first boutique under the brand name Sacha, a Russian abbreviation of Alexander, which means 'protector'. Sacha shoes are designed for young and edgy fashion followers.

SACHA LONDON

Manufacturer founded in London in the late 1950s, named after the émigré founder's grandfather, 'Sacha'. The company came under Spanish ownership and operation in 1988 but the original name was retained. Its other labels include Sacha Too (sport and casual shoes) and Sachelle, a less expensive line.

RUSSELL & BROMLEY
Above **Advertisement for Russell & Bromley, Spring 1976**

SACHA LONDON
Right **Suede appliquéd pump, late 1980s**

RUTHIE DAVIS
Opposite **Three colourfully trimmed patent leather stiletto-heeled shoes, Autumn/Winter 2009**

SALAMANDER

Jakob Sigle founded a manufacturing company in Kornwestheim, near Stuttgart, in 1885. It was later renamed Salamander. In 1960 Salamander expanded into France and in 1969 into Austria. It was Germany's largest shoe manufacturer, and at the peak of production in 1967 Salamander was producing 13.5 million pairs of shoes per year. By 1981 that number had fallen to 8 million pairs, but after German reunification in the 1990s Salamander expanded its business into the former East Germany as well as Czechoslovakia, Poland, Hungary and Russia. Salamander announced insolvency in 2004.

SALVATORE FERRAGAMO

Salvatore Ferragamo (1898–1960) was born in Italy and was apprenticed as a shoemaker. In 1914 he went to the United States and seriously studied all sides of his trade. He examined American methods of production, the chemistry of dyeing leather and the anatomy of the foot, and opened a small workshop to make shoes. He was fortunate to work in Santa Barbara as the film industry took off, and he won the admiration and patronage of film stars and Hollywood producers. He returned to Italy in 1927, where economic necessities made him turn to unconventional design solutions, including making platform shoes of wood and cork. After the war Salvatore continued to set design standards. His 1947 collection of shoes, for which he won a Neiman Marcus Award for Distinguished Service, was paired with Christian Dior's New Look collection, and featured a sandal with 'invisible' transparent nylon thread-like straps, a style still in fashion today. Ferragamo regained his role as shoemaker to the stars during the 1950s, when his clientele included royalty and Hollywood legends who would travel to his Florence headquarters, the medieval Palazzo Spini Feroni, to have bespoke shoes made by the master. His design innovations led to hundreds of patents, and he was one of the first shoe designers to make use of the incredibly slim stiletto heel in the 1950s. At the time of his death in

SALVATORE FERRAGAMO
Black suede low-heeled pumps with serrated topline, 1954

SALVATORE FERRAGAMO
Above **Black suede oxfords with white mink aglets, *c.* 1950**

Right **White suede monk-strap pumps, 1951**

1960 his workshop was producing 350 pairs of handmade shoes a day. Since his death the business has remained a family-owned enterprise. His daughter **FIAMMA FERRAGAMO** showed her first collection in London in 1961 and went on to build up the company throughout the 1990s. Ferragamo is now the largest Italian exporter of high-end footwear, producing over 10,000 pairs per day. In 2009 Vivia Ferragamo, Salvatore's granddaughter, launched a shoe collection for Liberty of London, and the company collaborated on a line of shoes with Japanese designer Yohji Yamamoto.

SAM & LIBBY

Sam Edelman was born into a family with a history of involvement in the leather tanning industry. His grandfather was a founding partner of the Fleming-Joffe reptile tannery that supplied exotic leathers to the shoe trade. After the tannery closed in 1976 Sam and his father, Arthur Edelman, opened their own business, which made the first shoe collection for Ralph Lauren. Arthur left the shoe trade to start a leather supply business, leaving Sam to develop with his wife Libby a shoe division for Esprit in 1985. In 1988 they launched their own brand called Sam & Libby. It started well, with a very successful ballet flat, but their subsequent additions did not match the promise. In 1996 their trademarks and trade names were sold to Maxwell Shoe.

SANDRO VICARI

Founded in 1960 near Venice, the company focuses on high-fashion footwear for sale through exclusive retailers around the world under the labels Sandro Vicari, Vicari and Linea Wallys.

SARA NOVARRO

Third-generation shoemaker, Sara Novarro was born in 1957. In 1979 she joined the design department of the family business, Komfort Spain, a high-volume shoe manufacturer. The Via Sara Novarro line, targeted at the export fashion market, was launched in 1988. Collaborative shoe collections followed, such as in 1992 for Martine Sitbon in Paris. She continues to design the Sara Novarro line, as well as the more accessible label Pretty Shoes.

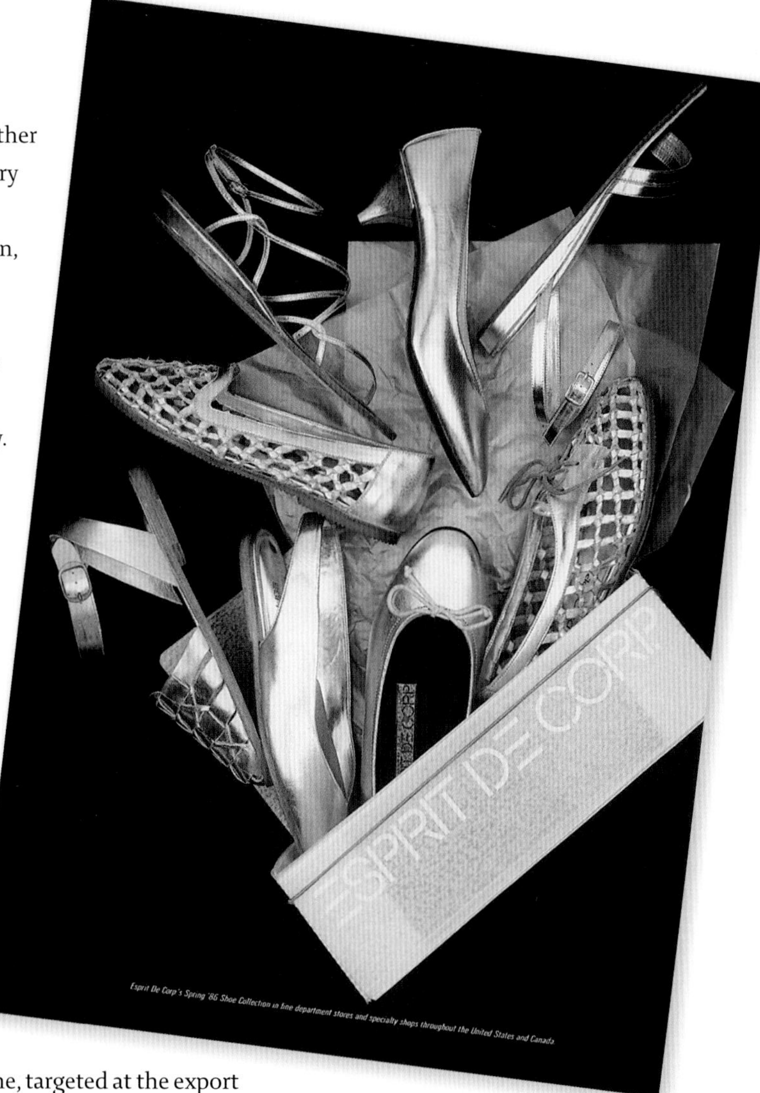

SAM & LIBBY
Advertisement for Sam & Libby Edelman shoe designs for Esprit, Winter 1985–86

SBICCA
Advertisement for Sbicca, Autumn 1957

SARKIS DER BALIAN

Born in Silicia, Armenia, Der Balian was orphaned when he was seven and raised by a shoemaker who taught him the craft. He arrived in Paris in 1929 and found freelance work as a shoe designer. In 1943 he opened his own workshop in Paris, soon moving to the rue Saint-Honoré. Over the years he received numerous awards and accolades for his work and made shoes for famous clients, including Marie Curie, Greta Garbo, Salvador Dalí, Lily Pons and Yehudi Menuhin. He continued to make shoes until 1995, the year before his death.

SAVAGE SHOES

Savage Shoes was formed from the merging of three companies in Preston, Ontario, in the late 1930s. Other local companies were absorbed in the 1940s. By 1963 Medcalf Shoes and Scroggins Shoe Company had been added. The company produced mostly women's and children's cemented shoes under the labels Amellos, Hi-Los, Hurlburt, Koolies, McHale, Melody, Natur-fit, Rand, Savage, Sensations and Teeners, as well as the Canadian production of the American brands **QUEEN QUALITY** and Vitality. The company closed in the late 1980s.

SBICCA

Founders Frank and Earnesta Sbicca were born and raised near each other in Italy, but didn't meet until after they emigrated to the United States. There they married and founded a company in Philadelphia in 1920 to make shoes by hand in their own living room. As production increased the company moved west to California in 1943 and the changed environment stimulated new designs, including sandals, for which they became known. The company is still under family ownership, though some production has moved offshore in recent years.

SCHLESS, EVELYN

New York shoe designer Evelyn Schless had been the editor of the trade magazine *Boot and Shoe Recorder* before taking up shoe design in 1964. She found almost immediate success and her name was soon associated with other luxury brand shoe designers like **DAVID EVINS** and **JERRY EDUOARD** until her sudden death in June 1968.

SCHWARTZ & BENJAMIN

Schwartz & Benjamin has manufactured shoes under other people's labels since it was founded in New York in 1923. In the 1950s it produced its own line of shoes under the name Customcraft, but under Arthur Schwartz, the son of the founder, the business principally became a leading import and distribution company and footwear licensee for prestigious brands. Over the years these have included Yves Saint Laurent, Givenchy, Anne Klein, Michael Kors, Juicy Couture, Diane von Furstenberg and Kate Spade. In the 1950s they produced their own line of shoes under the name Customcraft. The current CEO and grandson of the founder, Danny Schwartz, and his wife Barbara, the director of product development, started their own line of fashion footwear in 2005 under the label Daniblack.

SEBAGO

The Sebago-Moc company was founded in 1946 and developed a leather boat shoe in 1948. Sebago introduced the brands Jolly Rogers (1969), Docksides (1970, which became a huge fashion trend for the preppy look in 1980), Jesse Janes (1971), Campsides (1981) and Drysides (1994). **WOLVERINE WORLD WIDE** bought out Sebago in 2003.

Customcraft
The Dusted Calf—soft as cashmere, smooth as chamois.
Our own Velluto calf with just a suggestion of a grain.
The filigreed buckle set with rhinestones makes the
sparks fly on this mellow surface. Here it is three ways.
In a chorus of colors at the finest stores. Around $20.
Schwartz & Benjamin Inc. 112 West 34 Street New York 1

SCHWARTZ & BENJAMIN
Advertisement for Customcraft brand by Schwartz & Benjamin, Spring 1956

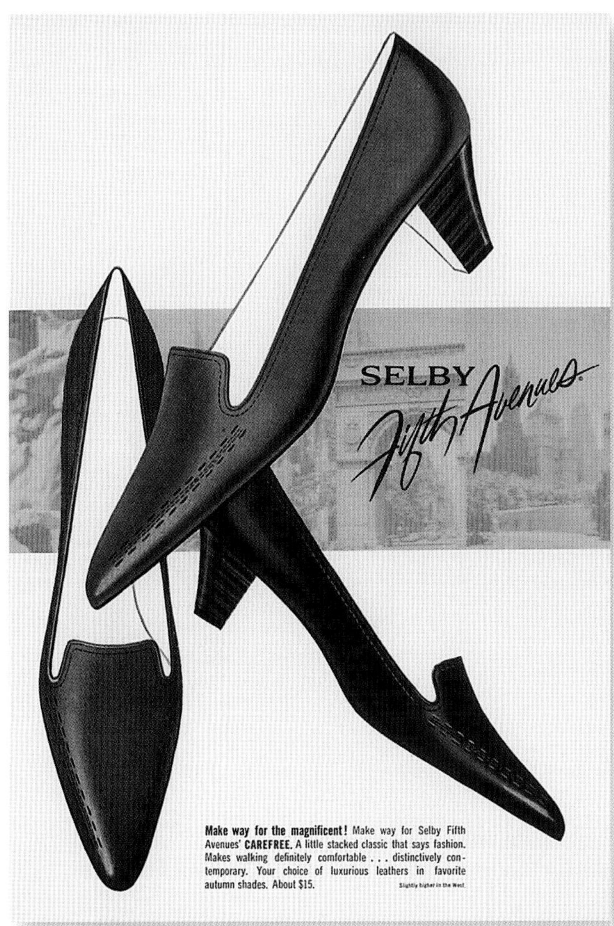

SELBY SHOE COMPANY

Having been founded in Portsmouth, Ohio, in 1869, Selby created the Arch Preserver brand of comfort fashion footwear in the 1920s. Arch Preserver cornered a large portion of the older American woman's fashion footwear market well into the 1950s. The company was acquired by **UNITED STATES SHOE COMPANY** in 1957 but Selby continued until it was closed in 2000 after the division was resold to **JONES APPAREL GROUP**.

SEMLER

Founded in 1863 in Pirmasens, Germany, by Carl Semler, the company made a wide range of shoes but became known for its women's high-fashion footwear by 1925. The factory was completely destroyed by an aerial attack in March 1945. Since its reconstruction, the company has since made only women's shoes, specializing in comfort casuals.

SELBY SHOE COMPANY
Advertisement for Selby Shoe Company, Autumn 1965

SEMLER
Advertisement for Semler, 2009

SERGIO ROSSI

Sergio learned the basics of his trade from his father, a shoemaker in Italy's Romagna region. Venturing to Milan, Sergio began selling his shoe designs to shops in Bologna in the summer of 1966. His first hit was a sandal called Opanca, which had a sole that curved up around the foot. Collaboration between Rossi and Gianni Versace developed in the 1970s. Sergio Rossi expanded in the 1980s and 1990s, and opened roughly two boutiques each year from Rome to Los Angeles. He collaborated with other designers, including Azzedine Alaïa and Dolce & Gabbana, with whom he worked for ten years beginning in 1989. In 1999 the **GUCCI GROUP** bought out Rossi, and in November 2005 Sergio retired. Edmundo Castillo became the creative director of the company in 2006, and Francesco Russo followed in 2009. Russo had previously designed footwear for Yves Saint Laurent and Miu Miu.

SERGIO ROSSI

Above left **Multi-coloured leather peep-toe ankle boot, Spring/Summer 2010**

Above **'Blush' patent snakeskin pump, Spring/Summer 2010**

SEYMOUR TROY

Born in Lódz, Poland, Seymour Troy went to the US as a child in 1910. In 1923 he opened a small factory making shoes under the attractively foreign-looking name YRTO. Eventually he produced custom shoes under his own name as well as a ready-made collection under the name Troylings. He was known for asymmetric strap closures in the late 1920s. He was given the first Mercury Award of the National Shoe Industry Association in 1960 in recognition of thirty-five years of pioneering design. Seymour Troy died in 1975. His shoes balanced high fashion with practicality, for example a high-heeled black suede pump with striking cuts and details.

SERGIO ROSSI
Gold sequinned satin gladiator sandal, Spring/Summer 2010

SEYMOUR TROY
Advertisement for Seymour Troy, Autumn 1965

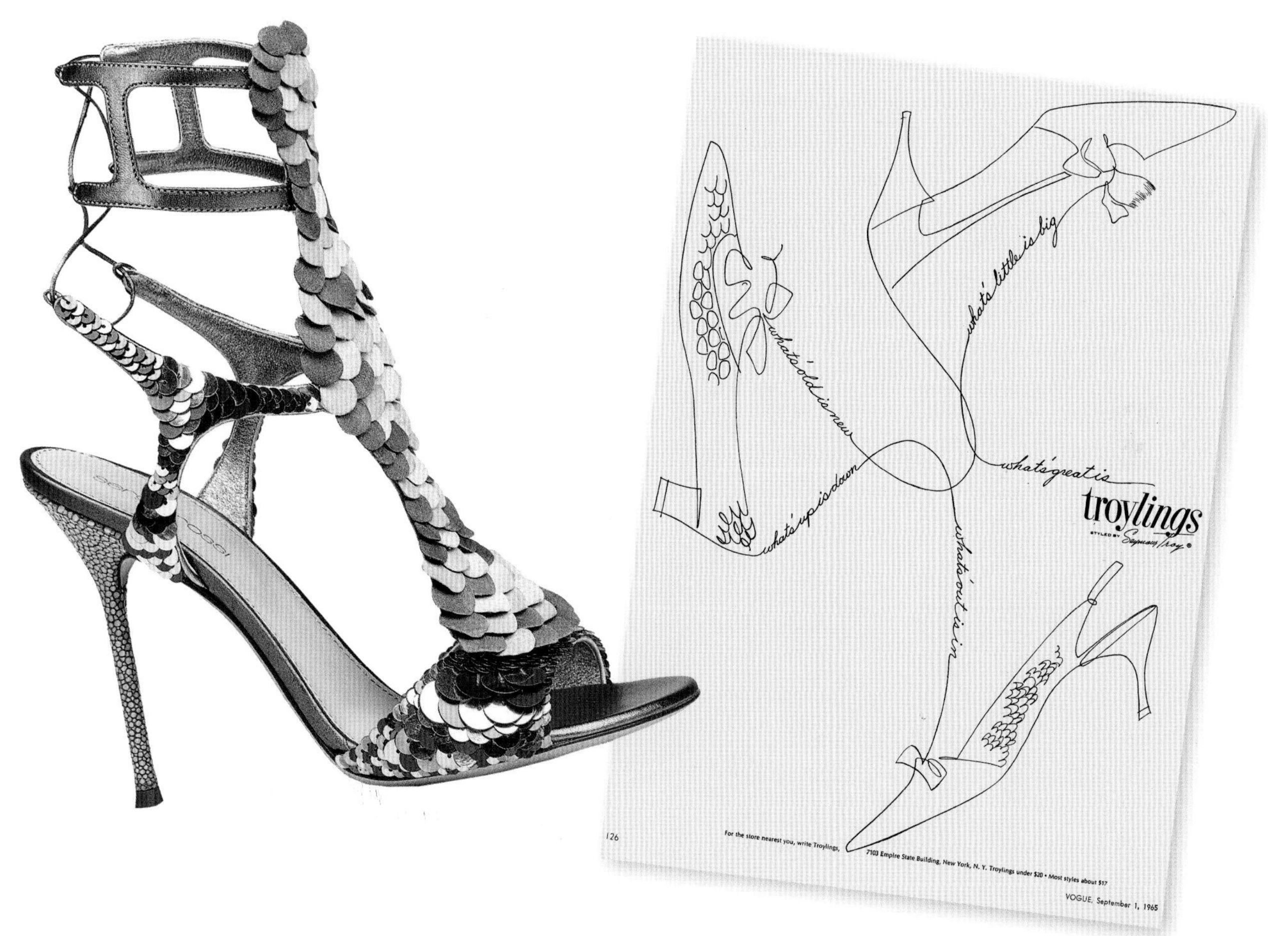

what's old is new
what's up is down
what's little is big
what's great is
what's out is in
troylings
126
For the store nearest you, write Troylings,
7103 Empire State Building, New York, N. Y. Troylings under $20 • Most styles about $17
VOGUE, September 1, 1965

SHY

Founded near Venice in 2001, Shy specializes in producing upmarket shoes and handbags that are sold through retailers from Moscow to Hong Kong.

SIDONIE LARIZZI

Born in Algeria in 1942, Sidonie Larizzi began designing shoes for couturiers in Paris in 1978. She creates bespoke shoes, mostly for individual clients and for shows, but also has a ready-made line.

SIGERSON MORRISON

Kari Sigerson met Miranda Morrison in a design class at the Fashion Institute of Technology in New York. They opened Sigerson Morrison in 1991, handmaking shoes in a small studio in Manhattan. Bergdorf Goodman carried their shoes in 1992 and demand built so quickly that by 1995 production was relocated to northern Italy.

SILVIA FIORENTINA

Silvia Sappia Baldi, who started the Fiorentina line in 1957, uses the name Silvia Fiorentina professionally. She was one of the pioneer American designers who went to Italy to have her shoes manufactured and had a longtime arrangement with Bergdorf Goodman in New York to carry her line.

SIGERSON MORRISON
Above **Black and gold leather flat sandals with tie-detail ankle cuffs, 2009**

Left **Metallic gold leather flat sandals with multiple straps, 2009**

SIDONIE LARIZZI
Advertisement for Sidonie Larrizzi, Winter 1985–86

SIGERSON MORRISON
Black leather knee-high boots with press-stud fastening at the sides, 2009

SIMPLE SHOES

Manufacturer founded in 1991 by Eric Meyer to produce an alternative to over-designed hi-tech hyped-up brand footwear. The company was sold to **DECKERS** in 1993 and became the eco-friendly division of the company in 2004, when Simple Shoes began using sustainable and recycled materials. Brands include the all-natural Green Toe (2005), Eco Sneaks (2007) and the more upscale PlanetWalkers (2008).

SIOUX

Founded in 1954 in Ludwigsburg, Germany, Walheimer Shoe Company began making a brand of moccasin called Sioux. The brands Autoped, introduced in 1957, and Grasshopper, introduced in 1964 followed its success, and by 1968 the company was producing over a million pairs of shoes per year. In 1998 Sioux acquired Apollo, a company known for its men's dress shoes, and in 2007 it acquired the licence to manufacture footwear under the brand JOOP!

SKECHERS

Founded in 1992 in Manhattan Beach, California, as a distributor of Doc Marten-style utility boots and skateboarder shoes, the company began producing its own lines of casual and active wear in 1995.

SOFFT *see* **H. H. BROWN**

STARLET

In 1945 Salvatore Anastasio began making women's fashion footwear in Naples. In 1957 his five sons joined the company and in 1972 they started a factory to make shoes under the name Starlet, mostly for the domestic market.

STEPHANE KÉLIAN

Stephane Keloglanian's family was Armenian, but settled in Romans, France, to work in the shoe industry in the 1920s. His older brothers, Georges and Gerard Keloglanian, opened a shoe factory in 1960. In 1978 Stephane launched his first women's collection under the label Stephane Kélian and he quickly became known for his high-quality, handmade woven uppers. The company has produced shoes under licence for **MAUD FRIZON**, Claude Montana, Jean Paul Gaultier and Issey Miyake. In 1994 the Fashion Footwear Association of New York presented Kélian with the Fashion Medal of Honor. In 1995 Kélian resigned as chairman of the company but remained as a consultant working with the design team until 2005 when the company liquidated its assets.

STEPHANE KÉLIAN
White woven leather pumps with contrast toes, counters and heels, mid-1980s

STEVE MADDEN

Steve Madden began designing shoes in Queens, New York, in 1990. Experience in retailing gave him insight into predicting trends, and in the early 1990s he introduced platform-soled shoes based upon 1970s rock and roll styles, which proved to be a great success. The first Steve Madden store opened in early 1993, and by December of the same year the company had gone public. By 1997 there were seventeen stores, which also included a clothing range. In 2000 Madden was indicted for manipulation of the company's stock prices and was imprisoned for thirty-one months. The company, however, remained strong and continued to expand. Madden is no longer the CEO of his eponymous company, but he continues to work as its creative director.

STRIDE RITE *see* COLLECTIVE BRANDS

STUART WEITZMAN

Above Rhinestone-trimmed black textile evening sandals, late 1990s

Right Advertisement for Stuart Weitzman, Autumn 1993

STUART WEITZMAN

Seymour Weitzman was born in 1941, the son of Seymour Weitzman, who made the Mr. Seymour brand of ladies' shoes. During summer breaks from the Wharton Business School Stuart cut patterns for Mr. Seymour, and in 1965 he created an oxford with a bow on the vamp. The style was an immediate success, and when his father died later that year Stuart took over design and sales for the company, with his brother Warren overseeing manufacturing. Mr. Seymour was sold to Caressa Inc. in 1971 and production moved to Spain, where Stuart supervised the division with continued success. His clear Lucite Cinderella pump of 1982, for example, sold more than 70,000 pairs. Weitzman created evening shoes featuring Swarovski crystals, reviving a style popularized by Herman **DELMAN** and **BETH LEVINE** in the 1950s. Weitzman bought back the company in 1986 and renamed it Stuart Weitzman and Co. His excellence and innovation in bridal footwear – such as the Sheer Delight pump, with embroidered lace – brought him an IRIS award in 1987 from *Brides* magazine. He began opening his own stores in the US in the 1990s, and was a leader of retro-style footwear. In 1993 he repopularized the Louis heel pump and boot, and in 1995 reintroduced a sixties-style square-toed low-heeled pump. Weitzman launched his first handbag collection in 2007, and in 2008 he showed his first collection of children's shoes.

STUART WEITZMAN
Black lace and satin shoes, mid-1980s

SUSAN BENNIS *see* **WARREN EDWARDS**

TAJ

Shoes labelled Taj of India were popular in the early and middle 1960s and are still admired by collectors. Though they were apparently embroidered in the US using eastern silks, the manufacturer is obscure. It has no connection with the Indian chain store Taj, which sells western-style footwear.

TAJ
Embroidered cream silk pumps, early 1960s

TAJ
Advertisement for Taj, Autumn 1961

TAMARA HENRIQUES
Toile-printed rubber boot, 2004

TAMANO NAGASHIMA

Japanese-born Tamano Nagashima designs footwear for women that is made by hand in Japan and sold through his shop in Paris. His shoes often use non-traditional materials, such as plaited heavy cord, for a distinctive wearable art look.

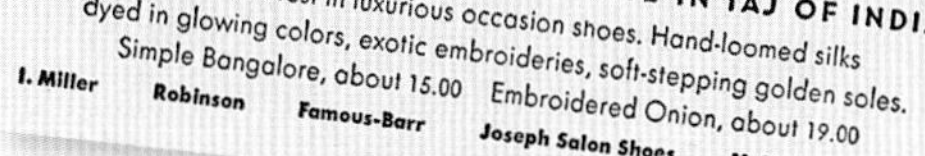

Taj
OF INDIA
THERE'S MORE THAN MEETS THE EYE IN TAJ OF INDIA
East meets West in luxurious occasion shoes. Hand-loomed silks
dyed in glowing colors, exotic embroideries, soft-stepping golden soles.
Simple Bangalore, about 15.00 Embroidered Onion, about 19.00
I. Miller Robinson Famous-Barr Joseph Salon Shoes M. McInerny, Honolulu

TAMARA HENRIQUES

While working at American *Vogue*, Tamara Henriques was introduced to a process in a Hong Kong shoe factory that allowed printing onto rubber boots. Tamara spotted the fashion potential and began with a floral-printed wellington boot in May 2000. Soon she was designing her own line of patterned boots, as well as for Thomas Pink and Paul Smith.

TANIA SPINELLI

American designer Tania Spinelli was born to Italian parents trained in tailoring and dressmaking. After studying fashion design at Philadelphia University she moved to Brazil with her husband. Her father-in-law was a shoemaker and inspired Spinelli to consider designing shoes. In 1998 Spinelli returned to the United States and began working at Tommy Hilfiger. She left Hilfiger to launch her own shoe line in February 2005.

TARYN ROSE

Created in 1998 by an orthopaedic surgeon, the Italian-made footwear brand Taryn Rose strives to blend the most fashionable looks with the best function. In 2002 a men's line was added and in 2006 the brand Taryn was launched to appeal to a younger clientele.

TECNICA

The Italian company Tecnica first produced a winter sports boot in 1971, which became the Moonboot in 1978. It resembled the traditional Alaskan Eskimo boot construction, with no distinctive left or right shape and an outside lacing to pull the leg and upper tightly closed. Produced in high-tech nylon and rubber, and in an array of fashion colours, the boots became popular as a fashion item in the late 1970s.

TANIA SPINELLI
Cuffed leather biker sandal, 2009

TENTAZIONI

Manufacturer established in 1975 by Alessandro Lupetti and Ernesto Troiani in the Marche region of Italy, Tentazione has since 1983 specialized in the production of youthful shoe styles. The company uses ecologically responsible materials, such as vegetable-tanned leather.

TEODORI DIFFUSION

Manufacturer founded in the early 1970s in Porto Sant'Elpidio, Italy. Teodori Diffusion produces high-quality fashion footwear, primarily for export.

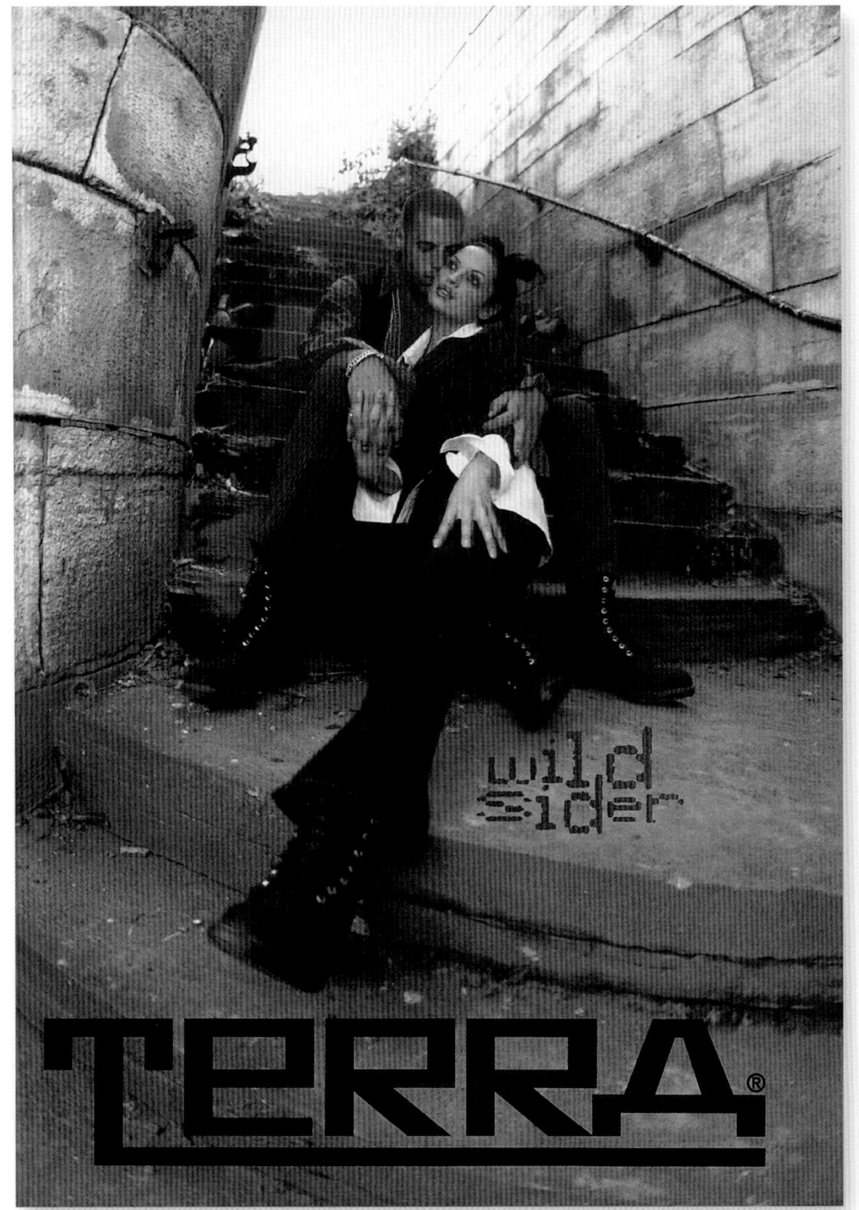

TERRA
Advertisement for industrial footwear turned fashion footwear by Terra, Autumn 1993

TERRA PLANA
'Janis' low-heel boot incorporating recycled quilts, with a one-piece sole made from natural latex rubber and recycled rice husks, Autumn/Winter 2009

TERRA

Founded in the mid-1970s in Harbour Grace, Newfoundland, Terra footwear produces safety boots. The trend for heavy-soled footwear in the 1990s expanded sales into the fashion world. Terra is now a division of J. Seigel Footwear, the same parent company as **MERRELL**, New Balance, and **CLARKS**.

TERRA PLANA

An eco-friendly design company originally founded in 1989 by Charles Berman. The company was relaunched in 2001 under Galahad Clark (of **CLARKS** family fame). He was joined in 2004 by designer Ajoy Sahu from Prada, and in 2005 by Asher Clark. All shoes are made from ecologically friendly materials by hand in studios that employ fair-trade principles.

TERRY DE HAVILLAND

Terry Higgins was born in 1939, and was apprenticed to his father, a shoemaker. He was living in Italy around 1960 when he changed his name to de Havilland. He returned to England and in the sixties worked with his father, making winkle-picker boots for men and women. When his father died in 1970 de Havilland took over the company and began making platform wedges in patchwork snakeskin, which he sold through **JOHNNY MOKE**'s Kensington boutique. The rock'n'roll crowd – including Bianca Jagger, Britt Ekland, Cher and Angie Bowie – loved the glamorous shoes, and sales took off. Tim Curry's shoes in the film *The Rocky Horror Picture Show* (1975) were made by de Havilland. As the platform began to wane in popularity, de Havilland led the return of the stiletto heel, first producing spike-heeled shoes for a Zandra Rhodes collection. In 1979 he launched a line called Kamikaze Shoes that featured winkle-picker stilettos

TERRY DE HAVILLAND
Green suede and snakeskin platform shoes, mid-1970s

TERRY DE HAVILLAND
Magic Shoes brand black platform boots designed by Terry de Havilland, mid-1990s

for the New Wave scene. When this venture closed in 1989, de Havilland began making shoes for the Magic Shoe Company in Camden, London, mostly for the goth and fetish market, as well as creating shoes for designers Alexander McQueen and Anna Sui. After suffering a heart attack in 2001, de Havilland closed his Camden shop and returned to his roots, revisiting his famous 1970s designs in both ready-to-wear and bespoke lines.

THIERRY RABOTIN
Left Suede and microfibre fabric shoes with a rubber wedge heel, Spring/Summer 2010

Below White leather Mary-Janes, Spring/Summer 2010

THAYER McNEIL

A chain of stores selling women's fashion footwear since the 1920s gave its name to a brand of shoes. The brand was dropped when the company's owner, Interco, which also owned **FLORSHEIM** and London Fog, sold it in 1996.

THIERRY RABOTIN

French designer Thierry Rabotin worked in fashion before turning his attention to footwear in 1978, since when he has designed shoes for **ROBERT CLERGERIE** and **TARYN ROSE**. In 1987 he founded an eponymous company with partners Giovanna Ceolini and Karlheinz Schlecht to create shoes whose comfort is essential to their design. Rabotin designs using the sacchetto method, which uses a single piece of leather for a shoe.

THOM McAN

In 1922 the Melville Shoe Company established a chain of retail stores named after the Scottish golfer Thomas McCann. Melville grew to become a conglomerate and between the 1950s and 1970s Thom McAn was one of the largest shoe chain retailers. By the 1990s it was the parent company of numerous other shoemakers and retailers, including Smart Step, Vanguard, Woodbridge Shoes and FootAction, as well as companies ranging from toys to pharmaceuticals. Melville divested itself of its shoe retailing in the mid-1990s with all brands reorganized under the Footstar Corporation. Thom McAn is now sold as a brand through the retailer Kmart.

THIERRY RABOTIN
Leather and suede beige wedge mules, c. 2008

TIMBERLAND

Timberland was originally a brand name of the Abingdon Shoe Company. The owner's sons, Sidney and Herman Swartz, had taken over the company in 1968 and in 1973 created a waterproof leather boot with a Goodyear bonded synthetic rubber sole. The boot was so successful that the firm changed its name to the Timberland Company in 1978 and opened its first store in 1986. The recreational footwear market soon became saturated and by 1994 the company was forced close its American factories and license production. In 1997 Timberland introduced a sneaker-boot hybrid.

TIMBERLAND
Advertisement for Timberland, Autumn 1989

TOKIO KUMAGAI
Black suede and gold kid evening shoes, mid-1980s

TOD'S *see* **DIEGO DELLA VALLE**

TOKIO KUMAGAI

Kumagai (1947–87) studied at Bunka Fukuso Gakuin, a Tokyo college of fashion. In 1970 he moved to Paris, where he worked Castelbajac, Rodier and Pierre d'Alby, among others. In 1979 he began hand-painting shoes, inspired by Wassily Kandinsky, Jackson Pollock and Piet Mondrian. Kumagai often altered the structure of his shoes to accommodate his painting. He opened his first boutique in 1980 but died at the age of forty.

TONI SALLOUM

Manufacturer established by Brazilian brothers Toni and George Salloum in January 1969. They began by making thirty pairs of men's shoes per day; its current daily output is about 2,000 pairs of men's and women's shoes.

TONY LAMA

Tony Lama, the son of Italian immigrants, founded his eponymous bootmaking company in 1911. By the 1930s he was supplying boots to Western-wear stores who were outfitting vacationers attending dude ranches, a popular holiday trend at the time for city slickers who wanted to experience the cowboy life. In 1961 Tony Lama moved to larger premises to enable the manufacture of up to 750 pairs of boots per day. Lama died in 1974, leaving the company in the care of his children. It was bought by the **JUSTIN BOOT COMPANY** in 1990. Tony Lama's name is synonymous with high-quality Western-style boots and shoes.

TONY MORA

The Mora factory was founded in 1918 in Majorca, Spain, but its production of American-style cowboy boots has only been around since the 1980s.

TONY LAMA
Women's cowboy boot styles, *c.* 2009

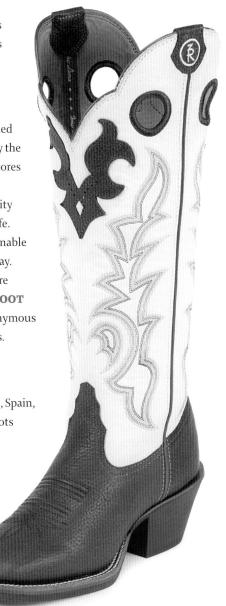

TOP-SIDER

Paul Sperry (1895–1982) was a pioneer in the design of the boat shoe. Observing that his dog had no difficulty with traction on the slippery deck of a boat, Sperry, who was a keen sailor, experimented to improve the rope- or rubber-soled canvas deck shoes of the 1930s. His design of a herringbone-patterned rubber sole led to a deal with the Converse Rubber Company to market a cheap and effective shoe in 1935. The classic boating shoe has been produced continuously to this day, despite takeovers by Uniroyal and Stride Rite in the 1970s.

TOSCANA CALZATURE

Founded in 1992 near San Miniato, Italy, the company has produced women's fashion footwear under the brand name Cafénoir since 1997. A man's line was launched in 2002.

TRIPPEN

Michael Oehler had been experimenting with the boundary between traditional shoemaking and wearable art while his partner Angela Spieth had been working as a freelance designer for different shoe firms when the two of them came across a cache of vintage shoe lasts in 1992. This was the catalyst for the founding of Trippen. The first collection premiered in a Berlin art gallery, and in 1995 Trippen opened its own showroom and shop in Berlin. There are now 450 shops worldwide stocking the brand, and Trippen shops across Japan, and in Cologne, London, Bilbao and Reykjavik. In 1996 Trippen won an award from the International Design Centre in Stuttgart and has since received many other international design awards.

TRIPPEN
'Zeus' black leather sandal-boot, 2009

TRIPPEN

Right 'Ibis' leather and feathers sandal-clog, 2009

Below 'Tango' beaded strappy leather sandal-clog, 2009

TWEEDIE FOOTWEAR

Manufacturer founded in Jefferson City, Missouri, as the Priesmeyer Shoe Company in 1874. John Tweedie and his son Charles successively led the company, which changed its name during the First World War to avoid prejudicial sentiments. The company was known for its gaiters and leggings and also produced a line of mid-priced walking shoes.

UGG

Company created in 1979 to import Australian sheepskin boots (*see* **WARMBAT**).

UNIC

Originally established by Joseph Fenestrier in Romans, France, in 1895 as a factory making rubber boots, Unic developed in the first half of the twentieth century as a successful maker of high-quality footwear for men and women. Throughout Europe, Russia and the Middle East there were Unic outlets, and figures such as **SARKIS DER BALIAN** were among its designers. During the Second World War the company had to adapt output to shoes made of substitute materials including wood, raffia and felt. After the war the connection with the Fenestrier family ceased and the business merged with Sirius before being taken over by **CHARLES JOURDAN** in 1969. In 1977 it was acquired by **ROBERT CLERGERIE**, who restructured Unic while continuing to produce a line of men's Goodyear-welted shoes under the Fenestrier label. Clergerie also produced a line of women's high-fashion boots and shoes under his own label.

Slanta
Tweedies
ALLURING FOOTWEAR®
the feminine slant
fastidiously
fashioned.
There is a dealer near you.
TWEEDIE FOOTWEAR CORPORATION · JEFFERSON CITY · MISSOURI

TWEEDIE FOOTWEAR
Advertisement for Tweedies, Autumn 1951

UGG
Classic short sheepskin boot, late 2000s

UNITED NUDE
'Möbius' shoe designed by Rem Koolhaas from a single strip of Kevlar to form the sole and instep, 2009

UNISA
Advertisement for Unisa, Winter 1997–98

UNISA

Founded in 1973, Unisa designs women's shoes, handbags and accessories sourced from Italy, Brazil, Spain and Asia for distribution throughout Europe and the Americas, as well as the Pacific rim.

UNITED NUDE

Established in 2003 by architect Rem Koolhaas and shoe manufacturer Galahad Clark, United Nude has grown into a collaboration of creative minds, including architects and designers. The design studios in London and production in Guangzhou, China, produce conspicuously contemporary shoes and boots that borrow design inspirations from sources such as furniture and architecture.

UNITED STATES SHOE CORPORATION

During the economic depression of the 1920s eight leading shoe manufacturers in Cincinnati, Ohio, merged to become the United States Shoe Corporation (USSC). The company relied for profits on volume sales of its footwear. Its **RED CROSS** brand was especially successful; despite difficulties with the use of a name associated with the international humanitarian organization, the brand continued to flourish into the 1960s. (The line was sold under the label Gold Cross outside the United States.) Starting in the 1950s, USSC began acquiring other popular shoe brands, beginning with Joyce Shoes in 1955, followed two years later by the **SELBY SHOE COMPANY**. At the same time it created its own brands, such as Cobbies and Socialites. By 1961 there were twelve factories making USSC lines. In 1962 the leading importer Marx & Newman, responsible for the **AMALFI** brand of Italian-made shoes since 1946, was added to the USSC holdings; Texas Boot was added in 1965. In 1970 the company set up foreign offices in Florence, Italy, and Alicante, Spain, and in 1978, Taiwan. With American shoe production shrinking in favour of cheaper imports due to labour costs, USSC began diversifying into clothing companies in the 1970s, and in the 1980s it bought the eyeglass chain store Lens Crafters. The only new line of shoes to be introduced was Easy Spirit in the late 1980s, which successfully aimed at working women who wanted comfortable heeled shoes. In 1995 **NINE WEST** bought out USSC, closed down much of the company's operations, and moved production to Brazil.

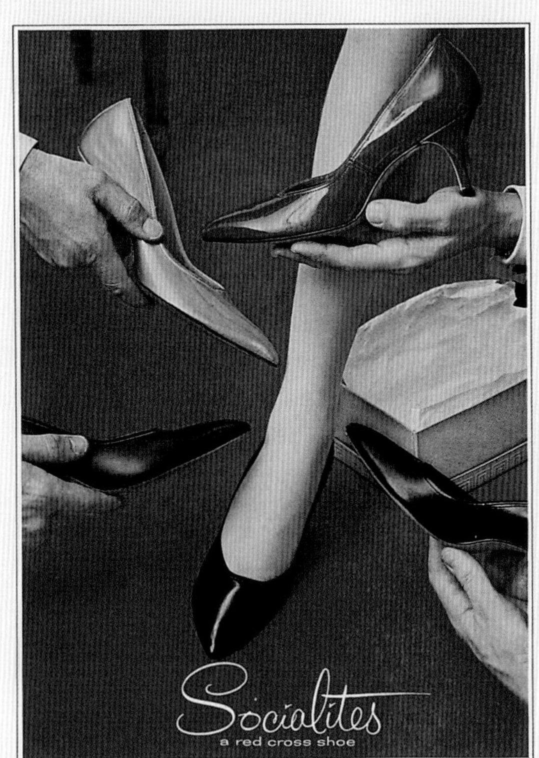

Socialites
a red cross shoe
FASHION FUNDAMENTAL . . . DISTINCTLY DIFFERENT
You'll know at a glance that this is the important new shaping of fashion's indispensable pump. You can see it in the pared-down sweep of the silhouette . . . the squared-off flattery of the throatline . . . the slim mid-heel that gives an illusion of more height. The difference is in what you don't see! It's Socialites' unique new mello-flex construction . . . that makes this the softest, lightest, most supple pump ever. Wear Square Top and feel completely pampered. You'll want it more ways than one! Socialites, 12.99 to 14.99
THIS PRODUCT HAS NO CONNECTION WHATEVER WITH THE AMERICAN NATIONAL RED CROSS • THE UNITED STATES SHOE CORPORATION, CINCINNATI 7, OHIO

UNITED STATES SHOE CORPORATION
Advertisement for Socialites brand footwear by United States Shoe Corporation, Winter 1962–63

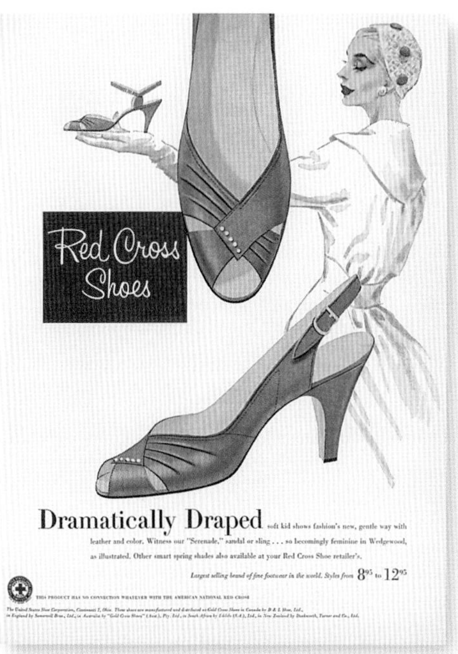

Red Cross Shoes
Dramatically Draped soft kid shows fashion's new, gentle way with leather and color. Witness our "Serenade," sandal or sling . . . so becomingly feminine in Wedgewood, as illustrated. Other smart spring shades also available at your Red Cross Shoe retailer's.
Largest selling brand of fine footwear in the world. Styles from 8.95 to 12.95
THIS PRODUCT HAS NO CONNECTION WHATEVER WITH THE AMERICAN NATIONAL RED CROSS

City Way Joyces – an urban quintet with street-right heel. Fully lasted on Joyce's new closed-toe Lark last for open-toe comfort! Of softest suede . . . they're city-wise for city-ways. No mail orders, please. Write, we'll tell you where. $11.50.

FIVE OF MANY JOYCES BUT ALL JOYCES SAY

joyce

PASADENA, CALIFORNIA

UNITED STATES SHOE CORPORATION

Above Advertisement for Red Cross brand shoes by United States Shoe Corporation, Spring 1956

Right Advertisement for Joyce brand shoes by United States Shoe Corporation, Autumn 1950

VAGABOND

Footwear company founded in the late 1960s in Sweden but operated almost entirely out of Italy. In 1994 Vagabond moved back to Sweden where all head office and design work was undertaken. Vagabond makes about two million pairs of shoes per year, with distribution in about thirty countries.

VALENTINO, MARIO

Mario Valentino's father, Vincenzo, had made shoes for Vittorio Emanuele II of Italy, as well as for Parisian cabaret sensation Josephine Baker. Mario carried on the family tradition when he founded his own shoemaking company in 1952 in Naples. In 1956 he expanded into making bags and leather accessories and in 1957 he began a contract with **I. MILLER** in New York, designing shoes for the American market. Valentino is credited with popularizing the stiletto heel as well as women's casual moccasins. A trademark dispute with fashion and accessories maker Valentino Garavani in the 1960s was settled only in 1979, when Mario Valentino was guaranteed the right to use his name for shoes and leather goods. Today the company is under the direction of Mario's son Vincenzo and has its headquarters in Naples with a showroom in Milan.

VIA SPIGA *see* **BATTACCHI, PAOLO**

MARIO VALENTINO
Advertisement for Mario Valentino shoes, Autumn 1986

VIA UNO

Manufacturer founded in 1991 in Novo Hamburgo, Rio Grande do Sul, Brazil, producing women's fashionable and practical styles for walking and daywear.

VICENTE REY

Born in Galicia, Spain, Vicente Rey began studying costume designer for the theatre at a Barcelona design school, but his interest turned to shoes when he created a collection for his graduation project. Moving to Paris, Rey honed his skills with a master shoemaker before creating his first public collection for women in autumn 1999. He won several awards as a new designer in 2002 and 2003, and opened his own boutique in autumn 2004. In spring 2005 he presented his first men's collection.

VITTORIO RICCI
Advertisement for Vittorio Ricci, Spring 1983

VITTORIO RICCI

Vittorio Ricci began in New York as a brand of up-market Italian import footwear in the late 1970s. In 1988 the Marx & Newman division of **UNITED STATES SHOE CORPORATION** in Cincinnati acquired Vittorio Ricci and its cheaper label Divertente Studio. The Ricci name was revived in 1990 as Vittorio Ricci Studio. The label aimed at the 'investment dressing' market and production shifted to the Far East to keep the price affordable.

VOLTAN

Giovanni Luigi Voltan was born in Stra, near Venice, and moved to the United States. Working in different departments of a large shoemaking factory in Boston, he learned the American system for the industrial production of footwear. He returned to Stra with American machines and methods and within six years was employing over 400 workers to make a thousand pairs of shoes a day. Being able to undercut the price of traditional handmade shoes brought quick success to the company, which by the 1920s had thirty-five stores in northern and central Italy. Giovanni died in 1941. The company still exists, making mid-market fashion footwear.

VOLTAN
Below and opposite **Stacked leather and crêpe rubber-soled slip-on and laced shoes, early 1970s**

WALK-OVER *see* **GEORGE E. KEITH**

WALK THAT WALK

After an education at the Fashion Institute of Technology in New York, Nicolas Berney and Alain Demore gained experience in advertising and marketing before designing footwear. They launched their Walk That Walk brand in 2003 and have since also designed for Kickers. Their Italian-made designs use unusual materials such as shark skin, neoprene and rubberized canvas.

WALTER STEIGER

Walter Steiger was born in 1942 in Geneva, Switzerland, and followed the family tradition of shoemaking by an apprenticeship with Molinard Bottier at the age of sixteen. In 1962 he moved to Paris and began designing for **BALLY** until the Swinging Sixties scene drew him to London, where he designed shoes for Mary Quant. In 1967 he presented the first collection under his own name. The show was well received, especially by the American press, and he was soon commissioned to design shoes by the new Parisian couturier Emanuel Ungaro.

He was the first of many fashion designers for whom Steiger would create shoes, including Claude Montana, Karl Lagerfeld, Kenzo, Azzedine Alaïa, Bill Blass, Oscar de la Renta and Calvin Klein. Steiger had opened his first boutique in Paris in 1973 and in 1982 had a second in New York. Since 1986 he has created lived and worked in Ferrara, Italy.

WALTER STEIGER

Opposite far left **Platform black leather ankle boot, Autumn/Winter 2009**

Opposite **Knee-high boot with stiletto heel, Autumn/Winter 2009**

Right **Animal camouflage print sandal, Autumn/Winter 2009**

WILLY VAN ROOY

Fashion shot for Willy van Rooy shoes, 1988

WARREN EDWARDS
Right Advertisement for Susan Bennis Warren Edwards footwear and accessories, Autumn 1986

Below Advertisement for Susan Bennis Warren Edwards footwear and accessories, Autumn 1989

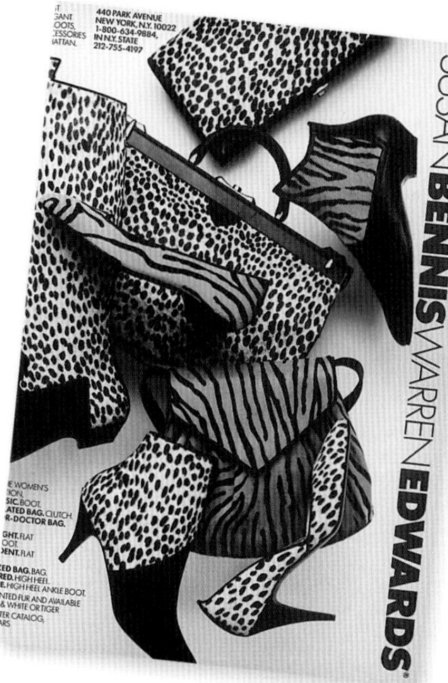

WARMBAT

Australian company founded in 1969 that produces sheepskin boots based on a traditional Australian style. The boots are better known in the US by the name of the export company, Ugg.

WARREN EDWARDS

Design and retail team Susan Bennis and Warren Edwards opened their shop in New York in 1973 with the goal of breaking into the high-fashion shoe market with Italian-made men's and women's shoes and accessories. The company was located on Park Avenue in the 1980s, when its distinctive styles brought it to prominence, but later moved to West 57th Street. In 1991 Bennis and Edwards opened a second store, in Los Angeles, but went their separate ways in the mid-1990s.

WICKED HEMP

Founded in 1997 and headquartered in New Hampshire, Wicked Hemp produces a green alternative of casual footwear for a vegan and eco-friendly clientele. Uppers are made of not only hemp, but also recycled plastic and wood pulp.

WILLY VAN ROOY

Fashion model Willy van Rooy started freelance designing in the late 1970s, selling her drawings of shoes and bags to Karl Lagerfeld and Yves Saint Laurent. When she retired from modelling in 1983, at the age of thirty, she moved to Madrid and began designing her flamboyant, richly coloured and detailed shoes full time. Her first shoes for the US market were exported in 1988.

WITTNER

In 1912 H. J. Wittner founded a family shoe store in Footscray, Australia, that has since become a chain of fifty stores. Alongside Wittner shoes, the company sold Dr Arnold Health Shoes, and grew by being the first to sell footwear in Australia by mail order. The third generation of Wittners now focuses on women's fashion footwear, selling the brands Zoe Wittner Design, ZWD, Wittner Italy and 7th Heaven.

WOHL *see* BROWN SHOE COMPANY

WOLFF SHOE COMPANY

Samuel Wolff founded the Wolff Shoe Company in Fenton, Missouri, in 1918. In 1949 Wolff bought a failing shoe factory in Washington, Missouri. There it produced women's fashion footwear under the brand name Deb Shoes from 1950 until 1971, when Wolff sold the factory and retired the brand. In 1986 Wolff shoe created the retail division Marmi, to carry its Barefoot Originals fashion comfort brand as well as the imported labels Vaneli and Sesto Meucci.

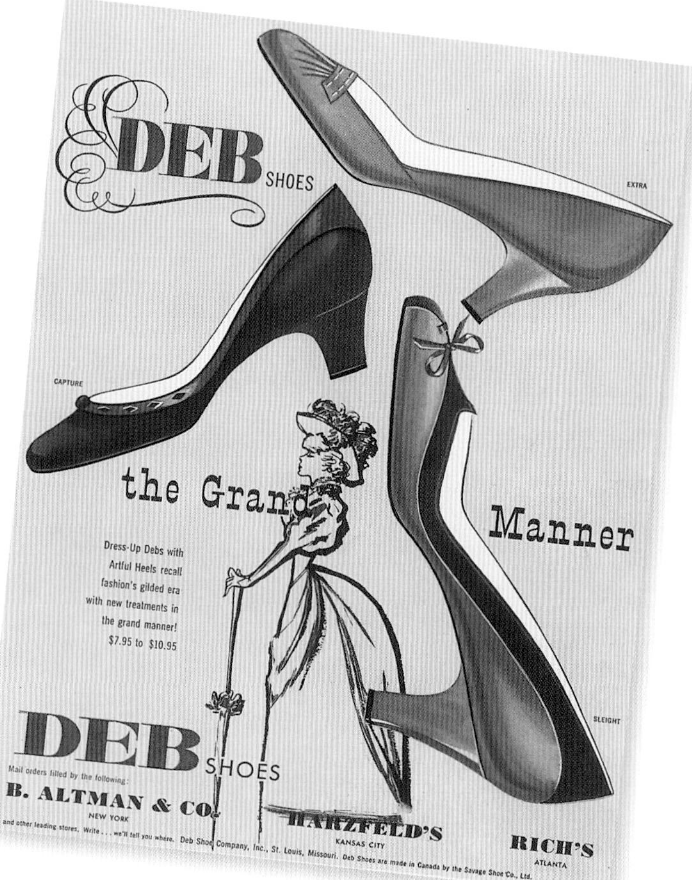

WOLFF SHOE COMPANY
Advertisement for Deb Shoes brand by Wolff Shoe Company, Summer 1952

WOLVERINE

In 1883 G. A. Krause and his uncle Fred Hirth founded a company to produce shoemaking goods. Out of this emerged the Wolverine Shoe and Tanning Corporation in 1921. In the late 1950s Adolph Krause, the grandson of the founder, was president of the company, just as the US government was encouraging the use of pigskin as an alternative to leather. **CLARKS** had recently introduced the casual Desert Boot, and Wolverine responded with a pigskin shoe with crêpe sole. The brand name Hush Puppies came from the company's sales manager

WOLVERINE

Right Shoe box for a pair of Hush Puppies brand shoes by Wolverine, *c.* 1960

Below Advertisement for Hush Puppies brand by Wolverine, Autumn 1998

who had seen some Southerners eating corn fritters, tossing bits to their barking dogs (coincidentally a slang term for sore feet) calling 'Hush, puppies'. The brand immediately caught on, and sales increased fivefold between 1958 and 1965, the year Wolverine World Wide went public. Sales for Hush Puppies softened in the late 1970s but the style enjoyed a revival in the mid 1990s, this time in bright ice-cream colours. Meanwhile, Wolverine started producing work and motorcycle boots in 1994 with an industrial brand called Cat, after Caterpillar construction equipment. Wolverine acquired the California company **SEBAGO** in 2003.

ZABOT

Berlin-based designer Julia Zapinsky has been working under the Zabot label since 2008, making contemporary interpretations of wooden-soled clogs.

ZABOT

Right and opposite **Fashion shots of Zabot clogs, Autumn 2009**

ZOCAL

Manufacturer founded in 1966 by Angelo Zoccarato in Padua, Italy. The company's intention was to create fine-quality women's footwear for export, using a combination of traditional craftsmanship and modern industrial production. The company is now under the direction of Angel's sons Diego and Chiara Zoccarato and their shoes are sold throughout Europe, Japan and the United States.

ZODIAC *see* **ENCORE**

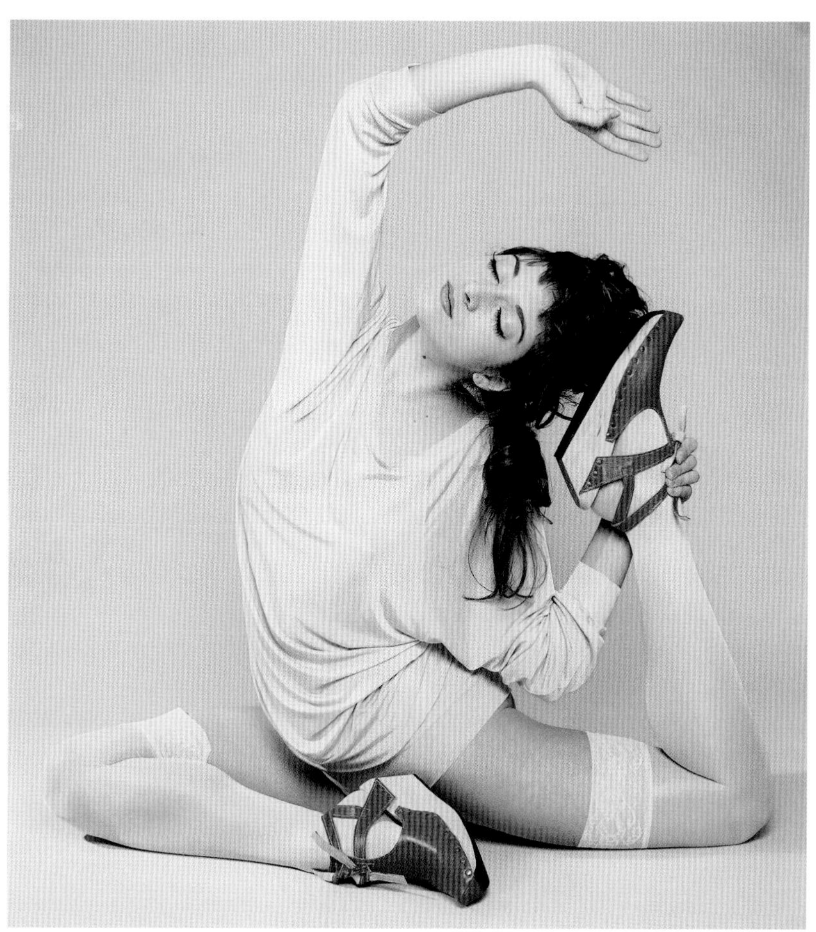

GLOSSARY THE NAMING OF SHOES

The terminology used in the shoe industry has diverse origins. It includes words used by ancient Roman shoemakers, such as sock and sandal, as well as terms from the Middle Ages, including cordwainer and mule. However, most shoe industry terms were defined in the nineteenth century, often named for a famous person or place – Wellington or Balmoral boots – and especially for inventors: Goodyear for his welt sewing machine and Pinet for his style of heels. With industrialization in the late nineteenth century, new words were created to describe new processes and parts, such as 'shank', a metal arch support used in the manufacture of heeled shoes. Once industrial production democratized footwear by providing affordable quality shoes for the masses, consumers pursued variety and novelty, the cornerstones of fashion. Fashion editors and advertisers, not always familiar with shoe-industry terms, coined words to describe and brand products. Many of these new names eventually became standard terminology. Sneaker, for example, was a slang term used by teenage boys as early as the 1890s; Keds adopted it for their rubber-soled tennis shoes in 1916, introducing the word into the American shoe lexicon. Around this same time spectator and Mary Jane also emerged, the former to describe a two-tone sporty shoe style, and the latter, pumps with straps. More names were added every decade, defining new materials, construction methods and designs. Some terms were universally adopted, like the 1950s stiletto heel, while others received limited regional use, such as brothel creepers, a 1950s English expression for men's heavy crêpe-soled shoes. By the 1960s brand names were even being borrowed to describe generic styles such as Doc Martens and Hush Puppies. More recently, fashion editors have created descriptive terms that appeal to a luxury lifestyle such as slides, limousine shoes and boulevard heels.

There have always been novelties in high-fashion footwear – a peculiar-shaped heel or unusual trim. In recent collections designers have begun to embrace a conspicuously contemporary style, abandoning historical references in their designs and often requiring new definitions. Since the 1990s footwear production has almost ceased in all previously prolific shoemaking countries except for Italy and Brazil, and production has largely shifted to Eastern Europe and East Asia. As the industry continues to grow and change, the shoe manufacturing lexicon will adapt to define new methods of production as well as new designs. Some of the jargon that describes today's high-fashion shoes will remain for centuries, but some might last for only as long as the style itself is fashionable.

PARTS OF THE SHOE

A shoe traditionally consists of a sole and upper, and the forward tip of both the sole and upper is called the toe. All toe styles are named for their shape, although the extremely pointed toe became known in England in the late 1950s as a **winkle-picker** because the toes looked sharp enough to extract winkles (edible sea snails) from their shells. The bottom part of the shoe consists of the heel and **sole**. The widest part of a shoe's sole is under the **ball** of the foot and is called the **tread**. A metal stud, called a **seg**, is often embedded at the toe to protect the tip of the sole from wear. The narrowest part of the sole under the arch of the foot is called the **waist**. The narrowest part of the heel is also called the waist. The **upper** is the entire top part of a shoe or boot, normally consisting of a vamp, quarters and lining. The **vamp** is the upper forepart of the shoe covering the toes and instep (the area of the foot from the rear of the toes to the front of the leg). Depending upon the cut of the vamp and where the seams are placed, there are different types of vamps including a whole vamp (the entire upper), a winged vamp, if the vamp is extended at the sides in a rounded shape towards the sole line, and an apron vamp, where there is a 'U' shaped insert on the top of the vamp, typically found on loafers and slippers. The **quarters** consist of the back half of a shoe's upper from where the vamp ends, usually defined by side seams. Frequently misidentified as the insole, a **sock** (in shoemaking terms) is a leather or textile **lining** glued to the insole to cover nail heads or stitching. Sometimes only a heel sock (where the heel rests) or half sock (covering from the heel to the ball) are used. The sock is usually where the label is printed or attached. To prevent the foot from slipping out, a small suede-covered pad is sometimes inserted inside the top of the back seam and is called a heel grip. Other parts of a shoe include the top edge of the shoe, called the **top line**, and the front edge of the opening of a shoe resting on the instep, called the **throat**. It is at the throat where a **tongue** is sometimes extended over the instep.

Beaded **winkle-picker** pumps, early 1960s

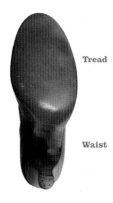

Tread

Waist

TYPES OF HEEL

The **heel** consists of the seat, breast, neck and top lift. The **seat** is immediately below the heel of the foot, the **breast** is the front surface under the sole, the **neck** is the face visible from the back, and the **top lift** (or top piece) is the bottom of the heel resting on the ground. **Stacked heels** are made from layers, or lifts, of leather, rubber or leatherboard that are fastened together with glue, nails or wooden pegs. All other heels are made from blocks of wood or plastic.

The **Cuban** heel, a term first used in about 1905, is a sensible low heel with a slight taper and broad width. A shapely mid-size heel known variously as a **French**, **Pompadour**, **hourglass**, **Louis**, **Pinet** or **spool** heel can be identified by its graceful curve and narrow waist. High thin heels were originally called **Italian** heels in the eighteenth century but when they were revived in the 1920s they were dubbed **Spanish** heels.

By the mid-1950s high heels could be made thinner thanks to the innovation of adding a metal reinforcement spike called a **stiletto**, named after the short-bladed weapon it resembled. A French shoe designer by the name of Charles Jordan (not to be confused with the more famous Charles Jourdan) was the first to use the metal reinforcing rod in his spike-heeled shoes, but many designers were quick to pick up on its use, including Salvatore Ferragamo and Roger Vivier, both of whom are often credited with the stiletto's invention. **Wedge** heels can be made from blocks or stacked layers, but the defining element is that the wedge extends forward to fill the space under the waist of the shoe, eliminating the need for a **shank** (a metal piece inserted between the sole and insole to keep the shape of the arch in a heeled shoe). Since 1950 a number of new styles of heels have emerged. The block heel with straight sides and a broad profile was introduced in the late 1960s.

Sling-back sandals with a carved and studded **neck**, mid-1950s

Leather pumps with **stacked heels**, early 1970s

Kid and elastic **pumps** with **Louis heel**, early 1990s

Mary Jane pumps with **stiletto heels**, late 1980s

Suede T-strap pumps with **wedge heels**, mid-1970s

Leather pumps with **cantilever heels**, early 1960s

Leather mule with **block heel**, early 1970s

Leather sandal with novelty **spring heel**, mid-1970s

In the late 1990s the blade heel was introduced – thin in profile like a stiletto but broad like a block heel when seen from the back. Numerous novelty heels have emerged over the years including the **cantilever**, **spring**, **orb** and **figural** styles.

TYPES OF SHOE

In its broadest definition, 'shoe' defines a variety of footwear constructions, including sandals, moccasins, mules and clogs.

The simplest and earliest footwear style is the **sandal**. As the Roman Empire declined in the fifth century, so too did the use of sandals. The style was re-introduced in the 1930s, however, and elegant and utilitarian sandals have returned as staples of the modern footwear wardrobe. Another early foot covering was the **moccasin**. Traditionally constructed from one or two pieces of deerskin with a soft sole, the construction is known by its Native American name even though a similar construction was historically used in Scandinavia and Eastern Europe.

In the 1930s a casual slip-on style of shoe called the **loafer** became popular. It incorporated moccasin construction but with an additional outer sole. Loafers often use a fringed fold-over tongue called a **kiltie**, a metal chain-link strap called a **snaffle**, or a wide instep strap across the throat that buckles on the outer side – a **monkstrap** – or a strap under which a coin could be slipped, inspiring the name **penny loafers** or **penny mocs**. In the US loafers are also sometimes known as **Weejuns**, a brand name (derived from Norwegian) made by Bass, since 1936.

In the nineteenth century a slipper referred to any finely made slip-on shoe

Sandal-clogs with **wedge heels**, early 1970s

Patent leather loafers with metal chain **snaffles**, late 1960s

Leather moccasin, late 2000s

Leather mules, early 2000s

Suede pumps, late 1950s

Leather Mary Jane pump and **sling-back pumps**, mid-1960s

for indoor use such as wedding or dancing slippers. During the twentieth century the definition gradually changed, and by the 1950s the term was synonymous with shoes intended for indoor comfort or bedroom use only. A **mule** was originally a backless, slip-on shoe intended for outdoor wear. The term originated from the Latin word *mulleus*, for reddish, and was coined for the red kidskin backless shoes made by the ancient Egyptian Copts. Mules were also called **slips** in the mid-nineteenth century and **slides** in the late twentieth century.

The term **pump** first appeared in England in the sixteenth century, but it is the Americans who continue to use this word when referring to a slip-on shoe; the British term changed to **court** during the nineteenth century. The exact origin and use of both words is unclear but court probably comes from the slip-on shoes worn by men at the royal court. A possible origin for the word pump is from the French *pompier*, for fireman. Apparently early Parisian shoemakers were often also fire fighters because they made the leather buckets for fire brigades.

A style of pump that comes back into fashion every so often is the **D'Orsay**. This heeled pump has the vamp and quarters curved downwards on both sides of the upper to the sole. Originally this was a man's slipper style but it was adapted for women's shoes in the late nineteenth century. It was especially popular in the 1930s, 1950s and 1980s. A **sling-back**, identified by the strap around the back of the ankle, has remained popular since it was originally created in the late 1930s. The flat-heeled **ballerina** has been up and down in popularity for casual wear since the style was introduced in the early 1940s. A woman's shoe held to the foot with the help of a strap is known as a bar shoe in England. American terminology for a bar is a strap, although strap shoe is rarely used unless referring to a **T-strap** pump. The name **Mary Janes** has been used in the US to refer to single bar or strap shoes since the 1920s.

A shoe with the upper comprised of overlaid parts (toecap, wings, counters, etc.) with decorative punching (holes) and sometimes gimping (saw-tooth edging) is often called a **brogue**. Similar in style, the **spectator** became popular in the early twentieth century for women to wear while watching summer sporting events. Spectators are usually light coloured with dark-coloured **toecaps**, **wings**, the sides of the vamp extending from the toe, and **counter**, the British term for exterior reinforcement or appliqué on the quarters of a shoe; the American term is heel foxing. The **saddle shoe** is a laced derby, which usually has a contrasting coloured 'saddle' across the instep. Saddle shoes were first made as men's golf shoes but became a quintessential part of unisex

Leather D'Orsay pump, late 1970s

Leather brogue, late 1960s

Leather spectators, mid-1980s

American teenage style in the middle of the twentieth century.

There are two kinds of laced shoe constructions. An **oxford** has a closed front (eyelet tabs stitched under the vamp) while a **derby** (also known as a Blucher oxford in the US) has open eyelet tabs, not stitched into the throat, but sitting on top of the vamp. Called shoestrings when they came into fashion in the 1790s, most textile laces use a tip to avoid fraying. When these tips are decorative, often sporting a tassel or bead, they are referred to as aglets, but when they are utilitarian metal or plastic they can be called either an **aglet** or a **tag**. Laces are threaded through holes that have various names according to how they are made. An **eyelet** is specifically a hole reinforced with a metal or plastic ring, un-reinforced holes are called **eyeholes** or **lace holes**, and holes bound with thread are called **worked eyelets** or **stitched lace holes**. **Blind eyelets** refer to holes reinforced with rings from the reverse so that the eyelet reinforcement is unseen. Eyelets or eyeholes appear on an **eyelet tab**, which is the extension of the quarters over the instep that bear the eyelets, unless the eyelets or eyeholes appear on **latchets**, which are straps extended from the quarters that do not quite touch and bear an eyehole each to be closed with a ribbon, lace or thong.

Leather derbies with **eyelet tab** sitting on top of the **vamp**, early 1950s

Leather oxford with **eyelet tab** stitched under the **vamp**, mid-1960s

Leather D'Orsay pumps wih instep **latchets**, mid-1970s

TYPES OF BOOT

Any footwear extending above the anklebone is called a boot. Boots coming up to the ankle have been called bootees or **ankle boots**. The part of the boot above the ankle that covers the calf and shin is known as the **leg**, or **top**, and sometimes **shaft**. Historically there have been many names applied to various boot styles: front-laced boots with closed eyelet tabs are called **Balmorals** after Balmoral Castle, Queen Victoria's Scottish estate, and **Bluchers**, laced-front boots with open eyelet tabs, are named for the Prussian general who, along with Wellington, defeated Napoleon at Waterloo. **Wellington** also had a boot named after him – a man's calf-length pull-on leather boot with side seams and straight cut top line. In the early nineteenth century this was the dandy's boot of choice, but the name is now mostly known for the unisex rubber boots used outdoors. When pull-on boots were introduced into women's wardrobes in the early 1920s they were called **Russian boots**, after Imperial Cossack styles. However, when they came back into fashion in the 1960s, they were simply known as **pull-on** or **stretch boots**. **Chelsea boots**, ankle boots with elastic webbing inserts over the ankles, were first produced in the 1840s and have been known by many different names over the years. In the early 1960s the Beatles wore a tall Cuban-heeled version, which became known as **Beatle boots**.

Ankle boots, late 1970s

Embroidered **Blucher boots**, early 1970s

Pull-on boots, mid-1970s

Satin zip-up **boots**, early 2000s

MATERIALS

Leather is a cured or tanned hide (large animal) or skin (small animal). The division between hide and skin is usually apparent but sometimes – such as with a calfskin – it is the pre-processed weight that determines the classification. In the UK 16 kg is the division between calfskin and cowhide, but weight definitions differ by country. Leather has two sides: the outer surface that originally bore the hair or fur is called the **grain**, and the inner surface is called the **flesh**. If a thick hide is cut into layers each layer is called a split. The tanning process prevents rot through the application of tanning agents, either vegetable (oak, willow bark, etc.) or mineral (chrome, alum, etc.). Chrome-tanned leather is occasionally referred to as **Vici**.

Suede is made from the grain side of leather and is sanded to raise the nap. The word suede was borrowed from the French word for Swede (for the common use of the velvety leather in Sweden.) The name was slowly adopted in the early twentieth century, displacing the early English word ooze. Suede resembles **buckskin**, which is the hide of a male deer. **Nubuck** is a brand name that also came to generically refer to all white or cream suede.

Painting the flesh side of leather with black varnish was originally called Japanned leather in the late eighteenth century. Seth Boyden patented an American improvement to the process in 1818 that used a linseed oil lacquer, and the process became known as **patent leather**. Today's patent finishes use a polyvinyl chloride coating that is less susceptible to changes in weather.

Patent leather derbies, early 1980s

Glacé kid pumps, mid-1980s

Boarded leather pumps, mid-1950s

Despite its name, **kid** leather is made from mature goats; leather made from kids (young goats) is too delicate for shoes. Sheepskin is also too fragile for shoemaking, but is often used to line boots and slippers. Glazed or **glacé kid** is kid leather with a highly polished surface, used for fine quality dress shoes. **Morocco** was originally a seventeenth-century term for goatskin from North Africa, dyed red from its sumac-tanning process, but, through common use, the term came to include any goatskin used for shoemaking that features the natural surface of kidskin. Crocodile and alligator leather are suitable for shoe uppers. They are similar in appearance except for a dot in the middle of each scale where a hair follicle once grew on a crocodile. Lizard and snake are fragile but are used as trims or are lined for strength. Often bovine leather is embossed or stamped with a pattern to imitate a different type of leather, such as crocodile. This is called **boarded leather** and should not be confused with **leatherboard** – a sheet material made from agglutinated shreds of leather and a binding agent, typically used for making lifts (layers) in stacked heels.

Neoprene soled **saddle shoes**, early 1950s

PVC 'wet look' **stretch boots**, early 1970s

Although the man-made materials rayon, celluloid, Bakelite and nylon revolutionized clothing production in the twentieth century, they had little impact on footwear. However, some lesser-known synthetics did transform the footwear industry. Polychloroprene, or synthetic rubber, better known as **Neoprene**, a trade name used by Dupont, was developed in 1931 and used as an adhesive in shoemaking as well as a soling composition. Many saddle shoes were made with Neoprene soles in the 1950s. **Neolite**, a synthetic resin rubber with excellent flexibility and wear resistance, was introduced as a leather sole substitute in about 1950 by the Goodyear Tire and Rubber Company. **Corfam**, a trade name used by Dupont for a synthetic upper material that reproduced most of the properties of leather, was aggressively marketed in the mid-1960s. Seventy-five million pairs of Corfam shoes were sold by 1969, but consumer response failed to meet expectations and Dupont ceased production. A Japanese company bought the rights and revolutionized the fashion industry in the 1970s with their refined version of Corfam called **ultrasuede**. **Polyurethane (PU)** and **Polyvinyl chloride (PVC)** have been widely used in the shoemaking industry since the 1960s. PU can be expanded into moulded flexible soles that are soft and light as well as wear- and slip-resistant. Laminated onto textile backings, both PU and PVC can imitate a variety of leather-like finishes. Although they are not necessarily cheaper than leather, they are more adaptable to mass- production methods. Their biggest drawback is that neither is permeable and can cause smelly feet. **Ethylene vinyl Acetate** is the most recent synthetic material used by the footwear industry, and is best known as the foam resin used to make the Crocs brand of sandals.

PU or **PVC vinyl boots**, mid-1960s

MANUFACTURING METHODS

There are four ways of sewing a shoe together. The **turnshoe** method sews a shoe inside out and then turns it the right way around. This ancient method requires a pliable sole material. A **stitchdown** construction, also known as a **veldtschoen** (Afrikaner for field shoe), sews through the upper and sole by hand or machine on the outside of the shoe. This is a simple method of construction but dampness can infiltrate through the stitch holes. The **Blake** or **McKay sewing machine** (named for the inventor Blake or financer McKay) was invented in 1858 and sews soles to uppers on the inside of the shoe. **Welt construction** was perfected over five hundred years ago. This complex hand-made construction attaches the upper and sole by sewing each to a welt, but through different stitch holes resulting in a watertight sole. Charles Goodyear invented the first machine capable of duplicating welt construction in the 1870s.

The idea of bonding the sole to the upper by means of an adhesive was considered in the nineteenth century but not put into use until the 1930s when lightweight, flexible-soled lady's dress shoes were first made using what is called **cement construction**. The cement process was a boon for European shoe manufacturers because they did not have to pay for the rights to use a patented machine or process like they did for Goodyear welting. A variation of this process called **California construction** uses a platform midsole between an inner and outer sole and was developed in the early 1940s for making women's and children's casual sandals.

With the introduction of synthetic plastics, moulding became a popular way of creating inexpensive footwear. There are three basic methods: **slush moulding** uses a dry-blend plastic compound poured into a heated mould until it gels; **injection moulding** forces a melted thermoplastic into a mould cavity, used for PVC shoes called **Jellies**; and **direct moulding** applies a sole of PVC or synthetic rubber directly onto a pre-made upper, commonly used in the production of athletic shoes.

California construction sandals, early 1950s

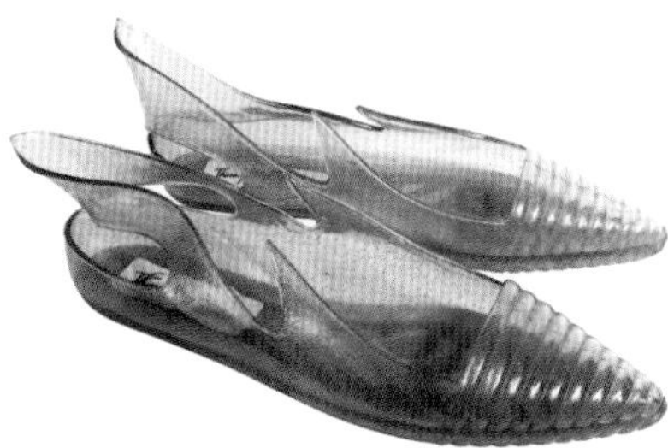

Slush-moulded jellies, mid-1980s

SHOE SIZING

In the eighteenth century shoes were the first items of apparel to be made for speculative sale. This was only made possible by the existence of a standardized **footwear sizing** system developed by English genealogist Randle Holme in 1688. His system defined a ¼ inch difference in length per shoe size, beginning with a hand measurement (4 in) as a child's size 0. After reaching size 12 the scale was started over again for an adult's size 0. Shoes using the Holmes system were sold in English shops as early as the 1760s, and the system still is the basis for shoe sizes in the British, American and German markets.

The French created the **Paris point** system in the late eighteenth century after the adoption of the metric system. Each Paris point equals an increment of two-thirds of a centimetre. This system is the most international in use, although a new system called **mondopoint** is gaining popularity. This sizing system consists of two numbers representing measurements in millimetres, the first for length and the second for width.

ACKNOWLEDGMENTS AND SOURCES OF ILLUSTRATIONS

This book would not have been possible without the generosity of so many companies, including designers and manufacturers, who graciously supplied advertisements, sketches or images of shoes from their archives for this publication. I especially want to thank two organizations that allowed me to use many images of shoes from their collections: The Seneca Fashion Resource Centre, Toronto, Canada, pp. 2, 18, 21, 29, 49, 159, 188–89, 197, 214, 225, 248 (carved lucite heels and suede wedge shoes), 250 (suede pumps and Mary Janes), 251 (brogues and oxford), and 253 (patent shoes and glacé pumps); and Shoe Icons, Moscow, Russia, (www.shoe-icons.com), pp. 38, 55, 73, 147, 151–52, 180, 189 and 193. Other individuals and organizations that generously allowed me to use images of shoes from their collections include Susan Langley, Syracuse, New York, USA, pp. 155 and 192 (pumps); Claus Jahnke, Vancouver, B.C., Canada, p. 183 (shoes); Ivan Sayers, Vancouver, B.C., Canada, p. 202; Peter Fox, p. 183 (boot); and The Fashion History Museum, Cambridge, Ontario, Canada, p. 193. The image on p. 115 is © Bata Shoe Museum, Toronto, Canada (2010). The image on p. 111 is courtesy of the Powerhouse Museum, Sydney, Australia © 2010, first published in *Stepping Out: Three Centuries of Shoes* (Sydney: Powerhouse Publishing, 1999). All other images are from my own collection.